About the Authors

Susan Brems spent twenty-five years as a Foreign Service Officer with the U.S. Agency for International Development, serving in several countries in Latin America, Africa and Asia. She earned her Ph.D. degrees from Johns Hopkins University. Fred Brems is an educator, researcher and photographer who held professional staff positions in U.S. embassies and schools, both in the U.S. and overseas. He has an M.A. from the University of Maryland. Susan and Fred reside in Durham, North Carolina.

Another Brazil Heard From

Voices and Insights from the Brazilian Countryside

Susan K. Brems and Fred G. Brems

Another Brazil Heard From

Voices and Insights from the Brazilian Countryside

Olympia Publishers
London

www.olympiapublishers.com
OLYMPIA PAPERBACK EDITION

A CIP catalogue record for this title is available from the British Library.

ISBN: 978-1-78830-237-1

First Published in 2024

Olympia Publishers
Tallis House
2 Tallis Street
London
EC4Y 0AB

Printed in Great Britain

Dedication

To the women and men of Upper and Lower Calos, who through their friendship, resourcefulness and resilience made our stay among them a success and our memories of them warm and lasting.

Acknowledgments

To our family members who saved the original letters; our relatives and friends who read drafts of the manuscript and always offered helpful comments; Dra. Enízia Fernandes, who aided us in countless ways throughout our time in Brazil; and Regina Maria Sousa, who was our constant friend in Brazil and in all the years since. The research itself was funded by the Population Council, the Social Science Research Council, the Inter-American Foundation and Johns Hopkins University.

Contents

The Second Six Months – Hitting Full Stride
July–December 1989 ....**99**

Map of Brazil

Preface

We wrote the letters presented here during 1989–1990, when we were living in a small community of Northeast Brazil. Susan had selected the community to conduct field research among rural women for her doctoral dissertation in social change and development and in anthropology. Once the fieldwork was completed, we returned to the U.S., and Susan joined the Foreign Service of the U.S. Agency for International Development. We subsequently spent twenty-five years living in seven developing countries in Latin America, Africa and Asia. Now retired, we found the original letters in the items sent to storage so many years ago. What began as a mere work of transcribing the letters for family history turned into a literary enterprise, as we relived the seventeen months we spent in a part of Brazil that is not widely known.

Though we have had scores of experiences in rural communities in developing countries since our time in Brazil, that first long-term experience remains vivid and special. Because that corner of the world is not what most people think of when they think of Brazil, we want to share our memories with readers. This is not the Brazil of Rio, with its famous beaches and hillside *favelas*, nor São Paulo, with its impressive size and commercial importance, nor the Amazon, with its flowing waters and tropical heat, nor even Salvador da Bahia or Recife, two large cities in the Northeast. It is the Brazil of the *sertão* – a vast, arid plain – and the *serra* – a small mountain range – in the state of

Ceará. It is the story of rural life under very meager conditions, the story of how a community that had never seen a foreigner put aside any misgivings and welcomed an American couple and their infant daughter. It is the story of how that American family came to embrace a new culture and become perfectly at home in circumstances radically different from the ones they were used to. More than thirty years later, we still miss that Brazil.

Renowned anthropologist Clifford Geertz famously stated, "Ethnographic findings are not privileged, just particular: another country heard from."[1] They have merit by virtue of their own specificity. Borrowing from Geertz, what we offer here is another Brazil heard from.

Certainly, people who have lived in rural areas in developing countries will relate to the experiences depicted here. We also hope the letters will interest students and practitioners of anthropology, public health and international development – and perhaps a wider general audience – by bringing to these pages a sense of the lives and resilience of the people, and particularly the women, of rural Ceará, Brazil. We hope the letters will encourage new researchers to undertake work in rural areas.

Though the letters do not go into the substance of the research, the idea was to see if fertility – the number of children women were having – was changing at all in a poor rural area like the one we lived in. Most population studies had shown that women began to have fewer children when living conditions were improving. Were lives getting better where we were, and were women having fewer children? Susan used the tools of both demography – statistics on the structure of the population – and

---

[1] Geertz, Clifford (1973). *The Interpretation of Cultures*. New York: Basic Books, Inc., p. 23. Ethnography is the description of the culture of a particular group.

sociocultural anthropology – the study of society and culture – to examine this topic. Susan and her teams conducted two five hundred-household fertility surveys. The final product was a case study that contributes to the body of knowledge in population studies.

The Setting

Brazil has five regions. The Northeast region forms that telltale eastern bulge on the map of South America (see map) and contains almost one-fifth of the nation's land, distributed among nine states. The Northeast alone would rank as the second most populous country in South America and the third largest in area.

Socioeconomic indicators were low at the time of the research and even today continue behind the rest of the country. The region's per capita income in 1980 was U.S. $800 equivalent, forty percent of the national figure. In Ceará, three out of every five people in the work force received one monthly minimum salary, which was about U.S. $55. Concentration of income among the upper classes was also greater in the Northeast than in Brazil as a whole: The bottom half of the population received eleven percent of the income, while the top half received the other eighty-nine percent.

Similarly, literacy was low. Only fifty-five percent of women were literate, as were only forty percent of rural women. Half of women ten years or older only had two years of schooling.

The regional development authority, SUDENE, estimated that only one out of every five people in the region had an adequate diet and that more than three out of every five children were malnourished.

By far the largest geographic area of the Northeast is the

sertão – a vast, hot, dry plain punctuated by groups of hills known as *serras*. Ceará is one of the poorest of the nine states and is principally composed of *sertão* and *serra*. It was in these locations, one *sertão* and one *serra* in the state of Ceará, that this research took place.

The parched soil on the *sertão* does not hold water well, and winter rains can be sudden, violent downpours. The *sertão* typically fluctuates between floods and droughts and is dominated by large cattle ranches. The *serras* that crisscross the *sertão* are greener and, because of altitude, cooler, but they are less accessible. The *serras* are divided into *sítios,* the word for the smaller landholdings that are best known for fruit, beans and cashew nuts.

The cooler *serra* supports insects not found in the *sertão*. All year round, insects are bothersome, but in the rainy winter months they are relentless. In part because of the biting insects, the *serra* is not a prime choice for year-round living. The mountains also make access more difficult, and when we were there roads were scarce. The few roads that did exist became impassable by late summer, when the dry earth turns to a fine dust that makes wheels spin like a car in a snowstorm.

The research sites themselves, known by the fictitious name of Calos in these pages, are two neighboring rural municipalities some distance from a regional market town of about seventy thousand people in the North of Ceará. The *serra* municipality is called here Upper Calos, and the *sertão* municipality Lower Calos. We call the regional market town Santa Rosa.

The best road in the area was a federal highway that linked Santa Rosa to the state capital of Fortaleza, some three to five hours (two hundred forty-six kilometers) away, depending on road conditions. While both Upper and Lower Calos are located fairly close to Santa Rosa, Lower Calos, fifteen kilometers away, was easily reached along an asphalted level road. The trip by car took twenty to thirty minutes. Upper Calos, twenty-seven kilometers away, was reached along a cobblestone road through the hills, which rise to an average height of over six hundred meters (about one thousand eight hundred and thirty feet). That ride was about forty-five minutes to the county seat, which was a *fim de linha* town, that is, the state road ended there. The county seats of the two towns were connected but by a much rougher cobblestone road that wound for seventeen kilometers along a narrower, more tortuous, less traveled and poorly maintained path. By private car, the direct route between the two county seats took about forty-five minutes.

According to the 1980 census, Lower Calos was roughly double the size of Upper Calos's population of ten thousand five hundred. Although both were small agricultural, trade and artisan communities, the population of Lower Calos was more concentrated: Two-thirds of the population lived in the county seat, while the other third was in six outlying districts. The districts had both village clusters and dispersed houses, often located on *fazendas,* or cattle ranches.

In contrast, less than one-fourth of the population of Upper Calos resided in the county seat, with the bulk of the population in the outlying districts. These were broken down into one hundred forty-one *sítios* or small landholdings. In some of these *sítios*, residents lived in village clusters; in others, the houses were dispersed.

In short, Upper Calos was more remote, less populated and more dispersed than Lower Calos. Because of climate, Upper Calos was richer in tropical fruits and cash crops like coffee, cashew nuts and sugarcane. Lower Calos was richer in cattle and other livestock suited to the *sertão*. In fact, the rainy-season insects of Upper Calos were so harsh on livestock that cattle could not live there year-round and were driven down to the *sertão* for the winter. Lower Calos also offered services not available in Upper Calos: a gasoline station, a bank, a physician and a daily market.

Work and Life

Socioeconomically, all Calos was an area officially rated as having a "very low" quality of life. The rural area around Santa Rosa ranked number eighteen among two hundred two areas in the Northeast – on a scale where number one represented the lowest quality of life. Its low development ranking and location deep in the interior of the Northeast made Calos an interesting place to study fertility.

January through June 1989 was the first phase of qualitative (anthropological) research; July 1989 through March 1990 was the quantitative (demographic) phase; and April–May 1990 marked the second qualitative phase, though aspects of both types of research were always ongoing.

We lived in Upper Calos, in a rented house in a *sítio* of dispersed houses. The area was populated by sharecroppers, most of whom lived on the land they took care of, residing in simple clay or stucco houses erected by the landowner. In some cases, people lived on their own residential plot of land, in houses they built themselves, and farmed on someone else's land. A few families had small holdings.

Many of the small landholdings also featured a *casa grande*, or manor house, which in fact consisted of a modest summer and weekend cabin for the landowner. Landowners typically visited the *serra* in the season of least bugs to seek refuge from the heat

22

of the *sertão* and to receive their part of the season's crop. In a few cases, where the landholdings were large and cash-cropping considerable, the *casa grande* was indeed a large manor house in the traditional style of the Northeast. Interspersed were newer, more modern houses that occupied little land and had no land for cultivation. These were built on property that had been subdivided, for the purpose of providing summer and weekend retreats for people with means from Santa Rosa and Fortaleza.

We could only survey Upper Calos in the summer, when the roads were passable. By October, when we were working on our final *sítios*, many roads were almost impassable. Our car got stuck more than once in deep, fine dust. Return visits in November had to be done by foot – a very time-consuming activity in a hilly area.

In Lower Calos, we had to complete the outlying districts in the sample before the arrival of winter rains, again for reasons of access. Achieving this was very difficult, but Susan was adamant that the very dispersed, rural women that are so often left out of surveys because of their inaccessibility not be skipped. The county seat itself of Lower Calos was completed during the winter rainy season, which was uncomfortable for the interviewers but not impossible.

The letters make repeated reference to certain themes: economic issues, car troubles, the education system, electrical power availability, communications and insects among them. We intentionally included the repetitions because we believe that showing how time-consuming and important these aspects of everyday life were in Calos, aspects that people in more developed countries may take for granted, helps explain how daily life can be a constant struggle of simple survival, leaving little opportunity for people to improve their lot. It also helps explain why so little research takes place in truly rural settings.

Starting Off

In late December 1988 we left Washington, D.C., for a flight to Miami and then on to Manaus, Brazil, a major city on the Amazon River. We then flew on to our initial destination, the coastal city of Fortaleza, capital of Ceará. We stayed in Fortaleza for a few weeks to acclimate ourselves to Brazil and hunt for a used car to buy. Once we had the car, we traveled to the research area to get a sense of conditions there, make local contacts and find a place to live. Returning to Fortaleza, we made final preparations to move to the interior of Ceará.

Though our newborn daughter, Romey, was with us throughout our time in Brazil, we have omitted most references to her in the letters, considering that an infant's development is of greater interest to the immediate family than to the casual reader. She was four months old when we arrived in Brazil. We have kept references to Romey that are useful in illustrating our life.

With Susan occupied by the research itself, Fred wrote more letters than Susan did, typically to his father or Susan's family. The letters began once we were established in a transit apartment in Fortaleza. Fred took all the photos in the book.

The letters were either written by hand or typed on a Tandy TRS-80 Model 100 computer with output to a small thermal printer that printed on a three-inch roll of thermal paper. Thanks to Susan's sisters and Fred's father, the letters were preserved over the years while we were living overseas. Susan transcribed them and edited them for this book, arranging selected segments into three time periods, then by theme and within each theme by the letter's date; accordingly, readers will find that topics reappear. Because both of us wrote letters and any theme in the book can include entries from either or both of us, we have put the letters in the third person or first person plural.

The First Six Months – The Thrill of a New Culture
January–June 1989

1: Learning to Cry

1/05/89: We are here in Fortaleza, in a short-term rental apartment near the beach. We arranged this lodging by mail, and at first they put us in the back of the building in a tiny studio basement apartment that was damp and had very little natural light. Fred came down with a respiratory ailment almost immediately. We made friends with the young woman who cleans our room every other day, and she told us that there were much nicer apartments in the building that were empty. She advised that you have to be vocal in Brazil to get decent treatment. Our American sense of making do without complaint was not going to get us into an apartment with the fresh air and light that would be healthier for an infant and more pleasant for all of us. We learned early the Brazilian saying *Quem não chora não mama* – "If you don't cry, you won't get to suckle." This seems roughly equivalent to our "The squeaky wheel gets the grease." So, we complained with the management until they moved us upstairs to a larger, two-room apartment in the front of the building. The difference was enormous.

We had no problem with mosquitoes as we passed through Manaus, where malaria is endemic outside the city, and in Fortaleza the ocean breeze seems to keep bugs away. So far, we are lucky in that regard.

Everyone loves Romey; her blonde hair and distinctive looks turn heads everywhere we go. She enjoys going out in the

29

evenings to the beach, which is one block away. Fred plays volleyball in pick-up games, and we stroll through the nightly open-air market, where a trained monkey does tricks.

The only things Romey cries to complain about are the sun and the heat. Temperatures in Fortaleza in January are usually in the nineties, and the sun is unrelenting. When we arrived, a garbage strike had been going on for six weeks during this, the hottest time of the year. Rats are a frequent sight. We are three degrees south of the equator. During the hottest part of the day, we keep Romey indoors in the bedroom, which has an air-conditioning unit, albeit a noisy one. The other room of our apartment has only window ventilation. We do have an indoor shower with one knob for water but no bathtub for Romey. One of us holds her in the shower while the other washes her. We have no hot water, but here you don't want it.

We have spoken on the phone to Dra. Enízia, Susan's friend in Santa Rosa, and she has a lead on a house for us in Upper Calos, the first of the two towns Susan is focusing on with her research. It has running water and indoor plumbing! The project for next week is to find a suitable used car to buy that is within our modest budget.

Susan does diapers by hand everyday with water we heat on the stove. Then she hangs them out on the line in the back of the apartment building, and the tropical sun makes them nice and clean and sweet smelling. It is easier to do diapers every day than to worry about storing the dirty ones. Also, if we were to take them to a laundry service, we would have to pay by weight, and wet diapers are heavy. Laundry service is not sustainable on our budget.

Much of our day in these early weeks, then, is taken up in Third-World housekeeping, which is much more time-intensive than in the U.S. With little else on our agenda right now while we get acclimated, it is fine and sort of fun after all the cerebral work Susan has done for the past year.

We have no phone, but we can receive calls in the guard's cabin in the parking lot. When we get a call, the guard comes upstairs to tell us, and we go out to his cabin. Just asking for the *americanos* is sufficient. We go by the name Brenes here since it's easier for people to say our name as two syllables.

1/11/89: This is going to be quite a year in Brazil for two reasons: hyperinflation and a presidential election. The dollar has gone from 1180 to 1320 *Cruzados* in ten days, a nine percent increase. Presidents are only allowed one six-year term. That sounds like an interesting concept.

An initial observation: There are no weathermen on the TV – because the heat is so constant. We asked the woman who cleans our apartment if Santa Rosa, the closest large town to Upper Calos, is cooler than Fortaleza. She replied, "I've never been any place where it isn't hot."

1/16/89: The economic situation is very volatile. Laundry that last week cost U.S. $5.99 equivalent this week cost U.S. $4.48.[2] That is how fast the black market (parallel market) in U.S. dollars grows in times of inflation. Last night, the president, José Sarney, made a major economic speech. A wage and price freeze will be in effect for three months. The *Cruzado*, the Brazilian monetary unit, has been replaced by the *Cruzado Novo* (abbreviated NCz). Already there is a bus-driver strike, so Fortaleza is much quieter today, since most people can't get to

---

[2] Figures cited in U.S. dollars are U.S. equivalent, based on the prevailing exchange rate on the date of the letter, generally on the parallel market.

work. The freeze really hurts workers because wage increases always lag behind price increases.

1/20/89: It took us two weeks to buy a car, but we finally bought a car today: a 1983 Volkswagen Voyage, akin to the Rabbit in the U.S., though slightly more "glamorous." It has a trunk rather than a hatchback, which we think is more secure. Interest here on car loans is one thousand six hundred percent, to cover inflation. They have Christmas Club-like consortia, and nobody owns the car they drive. Anyway, after ten days taking cabs everywhere, we decided to go back to a dealer we had stopped by last week, when he had nothing suitable. He had just gotten this car in from another state, which was good news. In Ceará, no one can take particularly good care of their car because the potholes are fierce. Cars here are more expensive than in the U.S. The total cost, with four tires included, was U.S. $3,583, while in the U.S. we sold our 1986 Olds for $3,900. Of course, there is no comparison between the two cars. This car is totally driven by alcohol, so that is something new for us to try. We were ready for this and were able to pay with cash to avoid paying a high interest rate.

On Tuesday we will go to the research area to line up a house to live in; we have leads on three already. We will have no heating bills to worry about, that's for sure.

An interesting economic note: Wages are based on a minimum salary, and in theory everyone gets a multiple of that. The woman who cleans our room gets one minimum salary per month, which amounts to $41.53. If she saves $1–$2 dollars per month, inflation wipes those savings out. If she is ill, she loses her wage for that day. So, even though prices are low here because of the labor-intensive nature of the country, sadly, it is the cheap labor that really pays for the low prices.

We go shopping at least three times a day, visiting as many as four stores – meat, beverage, vegetable, general – not counting drug stores. Everything takes more time here, and we are fortunate to have the time right now. Taking care of Romey and daily chores can easily take all our time.

1/31/89: Fred spent Super Bowl Sunday night watching – the Super Bowl! The Brazilian announcers, not knowing the game well, to fill the time said at least a dozen times, "The stadium is completely full," as if they had no clue why it would be full, and "This is the championship of American football, the Super Bowl, between the San Francisco 49ers and the Cincinnati Bengal Tigers." Still, we were grateful for the broadcast. A great game! Fred watched it all through mosquito netting, holding one of the antennae with his left hand (the right hand gave him forty-four players on the field!) and the other hand holding the channel knob still until three a.m. (We think we are two hours ahead of Eastern time right now.)

Our car runs well, with one exception. When we bought new tires, they gave us the old tubes from the original tires. It turns out their price is separate, but no one told us that. Any salesman worth his salt would have sold as much as he could. As a result, we had the first flat we've had in six years, and we only had one hundred fifty miles on the "new" tires!

2: A House with a Ceiling

2/01/89: We spent the last week of January visiting the two municipalities (roughly equivalent to counties) where Susan plans to do her comparative study, Upper Calos and Lower Calos. We got temporary quarters in the market town of Santa Rosa while we looked for a place to live in one or the other. Right now, we plan to split our time between the two municipalities. Finding a house was difficult, but we had lots of help from Dra. Enízia, the friend Susan made on her earlier, 1987 trip to Ceará, who is an excellent negotiator. We were a little taken aback when she asked us if we wanted a house with a ceiling! We didn't understand the difference between the words for ceiling and roof. Most houses in the interior of Ceará have only exposed rafters holding up the tile roof, which leads to leaks and showers of fine mists in the rainy season and animal infestations. Some families can afford to construct a stucco ceiling beneath the open tile roof to provide more protection. Once we understood the difference, we expressed a preference for a ceiling. The conversation made us realize that we take a lot for granted in the U.S.

Upper Calos, the more removed of the two municipalities, is nestled in high hills that some people call mountains. Much of the time it is in the clouds. It should be relatively "cool," even though it is only three degrees south of the equator. It is twenty-seven kilometers up a mountain road from Santa Rosa, with a good twenty-two kilometers being rough cobblestone. The car

34

door on the driver's side opened twice from vibrations on the way up the mountain. The Upper Calos town seat has about two thousand five hundred people and two or three town squares. The houses are stucco with tile roofs. When we arrived to look for houses, residents were slaughtering a huge hog in one square. Everybody who is anybody was there!

The entire population of Upper Calos in the most recent census was ten thousand five hundred, with eight thousand people in the rural areas. It is two hundred forty-six kilometers from Fortaleza. In fact, the road from Fortaleza stops in Upper Calos, with no through traffic possible.

Lower Calos is only fifteen kilometers from Santa Rosa and seventeen kilometers from Upper Calos. It is not in the mountains but rather on the *sertão*, the dry interior bush country characteristic of most of Ceará. It is much more a planned town on a grid system, rather than dictated by the quirks of mountain valleys, as is Upper Calos. Again, it has several town squares but much larger houses. Dra. Enízia seems to know everybody or knows who in town knows what's going on. One prospective landlord we met is refurbishing a house right on one of the squares, and she was willing to rent us either the house she is leaving or the new one. The town is on a good road, but it is quite a bit hotter than Upper Calos. The two are good comparative study towns. Although life isn't easy here, we're beginning to find a number of nice places where things seem to work well.

The good news is that we decided on a house to live in. It is in Upper Calos but not in the town proper. It is in the rural area, on a *sítio*, or small parcel of land about four miles from Upper Calos town. The house, which belongs to an absentee landlord, is white stucco with green trim and a red-tiled roof. It is about what we imagined would be the best possible living arrangement.

It has a beautiful, huge old mango tree in the front – the weeds down here are the expensive tropical plants we have in the States – and fruit trees everywhere, dropping fruit like the Garden of Eden. It has running water, a shower, inside plumbing, tile floors and – a stucco ceiling! All this, plus a security guard/handyman who lives in a house a short distance away (he watches two houses for the landlord) for $66 a month. We had a chance to buy a three-room house for $400, but it was too small. We will have beautiful mountain heights to the left and right as you walk out of the front door. It is going to be grand! We move in on February 12 or so. We will stay in Fortaleza until then.

3: Money Troubles, Part One

1/31/89: Here is what an uncertain economy does to money: Last week we spent U.S. $48.76 for a lot of stuff. This week it would have cost U.S. $39.58.

3/21/89: The dollar today buys $1.93 in Cruzados Novos (NCz). On February 28, the rate was $1.53. All prices are frozen. So much for the economic plan. It is all going to explode when the freeze is taken off. Some say that should happen soon.

4/08/89: When we were in Fortaleza, the dollar was fetching NCz$1.90; three days later it was fetching NCz$2.12 in Rio. We try to hold on to our dollars for as long as we can because we know inflation will increase their value.

4/17/89: Rumor has it that the currency, the *Cruzado Novo,* is going to be devalued tomorrow. It's already at NCz$2.35 to the dollar unofficially. The parallel market is supposed to be illegal, but they announce the parallel rates on the nightly news anyway.

6/19/89: We are in another round of inflation here, with another devaluation and the wage-price freeze off. The dollar still holds us in good stead. It used to be that NCz$10 was a lot of money, almost U.S. $10, but now that buys a lot less. So, you think you have changed sufficient U.S. dollars to NCz for a certain time period, but you quickly run out as the prices go up. It's like walking on a muddy lake bottom: you know when your feet are touching something sort of solid, but you're not quite sure what that is.

The trip to Fortaleza now takes six hours because of the shape the road is in. We have to go there to write checks or change a traveler's check. The road will be awful until they fix the roads in late August after the rains stop. In some parts the potholes are more than a foot deep and stretch from shoulder to shoulder. The large trucks swing out into the flat ground to either side of the road to avoid the potholes but make the "road" up to two hundred feet wide in parts. Going slowly on the road and seeing a huge truck pass you one hundred feet off to your right is disconcerting. The roads will eventually be fixed, but then it starts all over again in January.

There is a beer shortage here. Can you believe that?

4: *Carnaval* Shutdown

2/01/89: It is quite hot here in Fortaleza – in the mid- to upper-nineties every day and for the most part no air-conditioning. A large number of bugs, mostly flies and mosquitoes, add to the discomfort. People don't use screens because it cuts down on the breeze. And the breeze does not seem as effective as we had hoped early on. We sleep under mosquito netting. Even then we get a few bites every night. But we are getting used to it. Upper Calos will be cooler but promises to have even more bugs.

2/11/89: We did some celebrating for Mardi Gras. Brazil is world famous for its Mardi Gras – called *Carnaval* here. People start getting ready for it right after Christmas, and the whole thing culminates in parades with floats, costumes and dances. The entire country literally shuts down from the Friday before Ash Wednesday until the Thursday after Ash Wednesday. Even the newspapers don't get published. On Ash Wednesday, everyone rests out of necessity. The cities with the biggest celebrations are Rio, São Paulo, Recife and Salvador.

And *Carnaval* in Rio is on TV the whole time, too. Dancers join together in what are called samba schools. The schools practice for weeks before *Carnaval*. Then each samba school – consisting of two thousand to three thousand people per school – does a two-hour presentation of music, costumes and dancing. The processions start at nine p.m. on Saturday night and go until ten a.m. the next morning, repeating the same on Sunday, Monday and Tuesday nights.

Fortaleza doesn't have a parade but has something like a block dance on the oceanfront road. It started about seven p.m. on Tuesday and lasted until eight a.m. on Ash Wednesday. The music, which we could clearly hear in our apartment, was blaring all night long. We took Romey down to the block dance early in the evening, and all three of us danced around to the samba songs that are characteristic of *Carnaval*. We spent part of the week at a beach house about one hundred kilometers southeast of Fortaleza, getting away from all the noise of the festival. *Carnaval* is fun to watch from afar, but it is for a wilder crowd than ours. The beach was much more tranquil.

Carnaval is a major reason we have had to wait until mid-February to move to Upper Calos, even though we found the house in late January. Tomorrow we move out to our new home.

5: Moving In

2/15/89: We are in our house! After weeks dedicated to buying a car, finding a house, getting used to the climate, food, language, telephone and food delivery systems, making contacts, and getting our Brazilian identification cards, we are finally here in Upper Calos. It is a relief to get all that preparatory stuff behind us, since everything here takes so long to get accomplished. What might take only five minutes in the U.S. may take a day or two here. On the other hand, the time pressure here is not so great, perhaps because the heat means it can't get too great.

We are in our beautiful *sítio*, or small farmhouse, about six kilometers outside of the county seat of Upper Calos. We got here Tuesday at three p.m. The place was a mess, but we got local help, and the house is shaping up nicely. It is actually cool at night here, and the mosquitoes seem to be few so far. We have five different fruit trees in our front yard and beautiful wild birds and local domestic animals, which keep their distance. Bananas right outside our window!

We were a little dejected when we first saw the shape the house was in. It had been unoccupied for the past three years. Our greeter was a gigantic pig that apparently had been sleeping on the front porch every night. The giant lizard that lived in the house also gave us a start, but it just waddled on out of the house, and we never saw it again. The owner had promised to get the house all set, but it was obvious little had been done. When we arrived, though, he sent people over to help prepare it. They are a couple who are the *moradores* on his land and so have caretaking responsibilities for the two houses on his plot. *Moradores*, which literally means "dwellers," work an owner's land in a type of sharecropping system. The husband, Raimundo, wears a straw hat and appears to have all sorts of handyman skills. The wife, Teresa, her chiseled face and straight hair clear indications of the indigenous origins of Upper Calos, seems eager to please. Of course, we pitched in, and tonight the house is scrubbed clean, with the old stuff stored. It is even nicer than we thought it would be, though the night birds are pretty loud. There is one that sounds like a dripping faucet, which isn't too pleasant, but we're comfortable.

Our home is a typical Brazilian country house for small landowners. Its white stucco walls are accented by green window shutters and a red tile roof. The wooden slatted shutters are meant to be closed at dusk to keep out the bugs, moths and snakes, though that makes it dark as night inside. The house has a big covered veranda and lots of hooks all over to hang hammocks. We bought a hammock already and hooked it up. All the interior rooms likewise have sets of hooks built into the walls. The main room has three sets of hooks! Hammocks are used here for everything: beds, living room couches, baby holders and places to read or rest. Romey is slowly getting used to them; she didn't like them at first.

The house is a good size, with two bedrooms, another enclosed room that Susan will use as a study and a large living/dining room.

The veranda on the house is fifty feet long and twelve feet wide. The main bedroom is eighteen feet back from the veranda and ten feet wide. This makes the house thirty feet wide at one end. The bedroom has two windows, one facing the veranda and the other facing the road. The main room is a good size, thirteen feet by fourteen feet. What makes the house special are the veranda and the rural environs. It really is charming.

We have water from the tap, from a well on the premises, so we have indoor plumbing. The water looks good, but it's not worth taking any chances, though we wash our dishes in heated well water. But of course, we can't use the well water for drinking or cooking. We buy large (twenty-liter) containers of mineral water and set the container up like a water cooler. And we put some in the refrigerator for cool drinking water. It works out fine, and that is the practice all over Brazil. We boil all of Romey's bottles and bottle nipples in the mineral water for twenty minutes after each use. That is time-consuming, but we are getting used to the routine.

The house has electricity, but there are frequent brownouts and blackouts. We've experienced several just over the last hour or so. Last Wednesday, the lights were out for about six hours. Of course, the refrigerator goes off. That is troublesome, since ice melts and water drips on everything. We keep lots of candles handy.

We cook on a propane gas stove, which does not depend on electricity. We buy drums of gas from a small store about two kilometers toward Upper Calos town. This appears to be the only supplier in the area. We just hook one drum up and should be able to cook for about two weeks on it. Our greatest luxury is an electric shower head that heats the water as it passes through, which is actually very scary, but so far no shocks. We have no warm water anywhere else in the house.

After we had settled in a bit, Susan took Romey for a short spin down to the bottom of the incline that separates our house from the main road that heads on into Upper Calos town. On the roadside of the adjoining property is a modest store, called a *bodega* here. A woman with light-brown hair came out of the store, smiling and holding a broom. She greeted Susan and Romey in a very friendly manner, offering, "I have one, too." Susan didn't quite understand what she meant at first. The woman put aside her broom, which she said she had been using to kill rats in the store, and went into her house next door to the *bodega*. She came out with an infant son! Edmundinho is just about Romey's age of five months. This is how we met our neighbor, Naisa, as a rat-killing broom wielder.

Upper Calos is the first of the two study towns for comparison. We will probably be here for six to seven months. The best thing about Upper Calos is the climate. The temperature here in the hills is decidedly cooler than in Fortaleza, Santa Rosa or Lower Calos, the second study town. All of them are like ovens. The temperature in Upper Calos is more like September at home. That is a gigantic plus after the horrible heat we have experienced since our arrival. We can easily forgive other things, such as blackouts and frogs in the toilet.

We are now in the rainy season, and it rains for at least part of every day. Things are very damp, and nothing ever dries completely. This is somewhat of a problem with Romey's diapers. Clothes, books and other items are easily affected by mildew, called *mofo* here. If you wear something once and it isn't really dirty, you can't put it away for a second use. If you do, when you next take it out you will find it has mildew on it.

Every rain produces a fine mist in the kitchen, which does not have a ceiling. We have gotten used to it.

Roaming around our yard at various points in the day are pigs, chickens, roosters (which wake us up good and early every day), giant toads called *cururus,* dogs and cats. Four donkeys are kept on the other side of the fence right outside our back door.

Our yard has all sorts of tropical fruit trees: mango, banana, papaya, lime, guava, and some fruits we don't even know how to name in English. The house is up an incline about fifty yards off the road and about three miles from the town of Upper Calos itself. We could not find suitable housing in the town; none of the houses had ceilings, only the tile roof. At first, we were disappointed not to be right in town, but it may ultimately work out better, since we are getting to know a number of poor rural women who are *moradoras*. Through Teresa, the *moradora* on our land, we will be able to meet a lot of women of the same class, which is exactly the research group of greatest interest.

6: The *Bodega*, Our Convenience Store

2/17/89: We have a sunny, breezy day, with birds galore and sounds of the wind rustling the huge palm and banana leaves. Romey is asleep in the hammock. With Teresa in the house watching Romey, we went to explore what is possible to buy in our next-door *bodega*. The *bodega* is about ten feet by ten feet and has two doors in the front that allow for foot traffic and hanging out. It is mostly stocked with the local strong drink, *cachaça*, which is a rudimentary rum made from sugarcane. *Cachaça* sells for about sixty cents a bottle and is very strong. Today was a bread day (bread is delivered every other day), so we got our bread. In the late afternoon and evening, the *bodega* serves as the local bar and offers beer as well as *cachaça*. We asked the owner, our new neighbor, what hours he is open, and he said that if he is not in the store, we should just holler, and he will come and open up. His name is Alfredo, and his wife is Naisa, whom Susan met on our first day here. In addition to their infant son, they have two daughters and another son. Alfredo is a handsome man who appears to be a leader in our little community.

Operating a *bodega* is a typical way for folks to earn some extra income. The small businesses represent a step up in the social order and are usually run by enterprising people as a family affair. Rural areas are dotted with them. Some offer only the most

46

basic items – a few canned goods, dried fish, sugar, rice and beans – and of course the staple of *cachaça*. If the *bodega* has a refrigerator, it will have soft drinks and beer. In Upper Calos town, *bodegas* offer a wide variety of items, including fresh chickens once a week.

7: Getting to Know our Flora and Fauna

2/18/89: We are in our fourth day at our *sítio*, and it gets better organized and more comfortable every day. The hot shower is quite a device. A heater in the shower head is plugged into a socket above the pipe; this heats the water as it passes through. The device has three settings: off, summer and winter. We fill up Romey's bath from it, so she gets at least one nice bath a day. She uses a plastic bathtub that we bought in Santa Rosa and takes her bath on the veranda.

We wondered how to handle garbage, since there is no organized garbage pick-up. It turns out we don't need that at all. We consume much more fresh food and so have little packaging. Teresa and Raimundo's dog, Duque (Duke), comes at Fred's whistle to eagerly eat up any scraps we have left after meals, although he never comes close enough to be petted. And Teresa showed us an area out beyond our back door where there is a small clearing. A hole in the ground about eighteen inches in diameter and eight inches deep serves as a repository for what little garbage we have. Every so often Fred will burn the accumulated garbage. Problem solved.

Today we had bananas from four trees in our yard. They are smaller than those imported to the U.S. and sweeter, too. We also have a lemon tree out back; it has big green lemons now, but they should be ripe in two weeks. Two pigs walked up our driveway yesterday, saw Fred and took off. We have a goat out back, chickens down the hill and a few timid dogs. The gnats are a nuisance, but so far, we've avoided mosquitoes. Our life is like camping, where you don't leave crumbs of food around and trash is covered, so we have no flies or ants thus far. The shutters are built so that nothing squeezes in except gnats. We are going to have the fine mesh netting we brought with us made into screens for the bedrooms, so we can keep the shutters open at night for more ventilation. We may set up a screened area for dining outside, since the lights attract so many moths at night. Sometimes we just have a light on outside and eat romantically by candlelight inside, which works out well.

Beautiful birds abound here, but nobody knows their names. Perhaps when you are worried about eating and living, birdwatching becomes a luxury. One man told me that the Southern Cross was visible from here and then pointed at Orion.

8: Teachers Wanted – Apply Within

2/20/89: It is already Monday. The trip from our *sítio* to the market town of Santa Rosa takes at least half an hour, but it's rough. Fred did it this morning for supplies. We are almost to the point that we have all the necessities covered, though many of our "necessities" are luxuries by many Brazilians' standards. Our expenses should level out completely. We spent no money on Saturday. We anticipate many days like that. When we think about it, we spent some money every day in the U.S. Here there is no place to spend it. And it doesn't feel right to be "showy."

2/21/89: Susan drove the six kilometers into the town of Upper Calos this morning to introduce herself to the mayor, a courtesy call to let him know what she is doing here. And his support, if not outright cooperation, certainly opens doors. At first, she was taken aback at the number of people in the room with her and the mayor. Apparently, people come to plead their case for whatever their mission is in front of everyone else seeking an audience with the mayor. There are no secrets here! This was the first time Susan, who famously dislikes driving, has driven in three years! You can't get out of second gear on this road, and there's no traffic except some cows and, most importantly for Susan, there are no merges!

2/23/89: In her meeting with the mayor, Susan mentioned that Fred was a teacher. The mayor's face lit up. Well, this morning two officials from the school came to our house to introduce themselves and ask if Fred would be willing to mentor the English teacher and perhaps do some teaching himself. Interestingly, English is a required course in school. Fred showed some interest, so they talked further. Fred asked them what the pay might be, and the officials said the most they could offer was equivalent to U.S. $35 a month. Fred told them to keep their money for other purposes; he would be fine to do it for free. We don't need the little money the school system is able to pay. Susan's fellowships are enough to support us in our modest lifestyle here. And it turns out that a teacher's regular pay is $8 a month.

9: The First Day of School

3/06/89: Fred started teaching at the local primary and secondary schools here today and thoroughly enjoyed it. The classes are fun, and Fred's Portuguese will improve rapidly with the contact. The people are refreshingly close and friendly. Some of the old fun of teaching came back for him. Both the teacher he is mentoring, Professor Z., and the kids are thrilled to have an American teacher. Fred is a real curiosity – the first person from the U.S. they have ever met. It is a real pleasure to have such enthusiastic students. Today, Fred handed out American postage stamps that he has been collecting from letters we have received, and the kids were delighted. He taught two classes today and will do three more tomorrow, then four on Thursday night with students who spend the whole day in the fields. Night students attend class until ten thirty p.m., walk up to five or six miles home after class and then go back to work in the fields the next day. It is not an easy life.

Our culture has such an influence on the youth here, particularly the music, with the backdrop of "plenty" and "opportunity." There is a "reality" line – since all the students say they want to go to the States. The U.S. can be a great place, but it should not be an escape for people, an escape from making the place where they are better.

10: Getting Started on the Research

3/06/89: Susan's work is coming along well, though starting up is the most difficult part. She is aiming to work most with low-income women who are part of sharecropping families here. Right now, she is starting to design the study and find out what types of data are already available and what types she will have to collect herself. She is meeting a lot of people, getting lots of information and doing some quantitative analysis of health records. She has met the mayor, families, women in the town and rural areas, agronomists and health workers. She is gathering scattered information that she can focus in certain directions for further in-depth research for the dissertation and perhaps for other products. It's a little slow-going at the start, since she has to allow time to get to know people – and vice versa – before she can start asking very personal questions about fertility. She is also talking to lots of people about the politics and economy of the area and establishing relationships with women of all walks of life. She is confident that the study will work out in the long run, but now it is a little scary to be setting everything up.

This past Sunday, we were invited to lunch at the home of one of the largest landowners in the area. He had learned that there were Americans who had come to live here and sought us out to invite us. It was a real experience: a thirty-two-member upper-class family of landed gentry. They own a five-hundred-fifty-acre plantation that grows coffee, sugar cane, all sorts of fruits, cassava and black beans. From these they produce flour, *aguardente* (sugarcane liquor) and all sorts of sweets. They have eleven families of *moradores* on their land. The *moradores* are the type of sharecropping families that will be the focus of Susan's study here. It was a remarkably interesting day.

We are here in the rural area without TV, no newspaper, no way to know what is going on in the world. Once a week we go to Santa Rosa to pick up any mail that may have arrived at a friend's house and to buy food. We purchase the Brazilian equivalent of *Newsweek*, so we can get some idea of the larger world. Otherwise, it is pretty peaceful doing without all that. In many ways it is nice to adopt the slower pace of life here.

11: A Durkheimian Episode

3/10/89: We have a story to tell about Fred's shoes. Fred had stepped in something one of our local goats left behind, so he put his running shoes out to dry after he had washed them. He looked for them the next day and then searched the house. The shoes were gone! Fred mentioned this to Teresa, the *moradora* of this *sítio*, and waited to see what would happen. Three days later – voilà! The shoes showed up on the back steps. Word had spread via Naisa, the owner of the local *bodega,* that the shoes had been taken, that we were here to live as neighbors and that what had happened was a shame on the community. She spread the message to all her customers. And then the shoes reappeared right where they had been on the back step! People here need shoes – granted, not size twelve – but the shoes cost more than a month's wages for them. That they were returned shows a remarkably close community, its cohesion, pride and values. Everybody knows everybody else, and Teresa was ashamed to have something taken from her area of responsibility.

We had a hunch the shoes would be returned. Very little is ever stolen in this locale. The exception is animals during the time when the crops are growing; food is scarce and people are going hungry. Susan is calling the shoe incident a "Durkheimian episode," because of the theory of the French sociologist Emile Durkheim. He posited that society and culture influence people's behavior through shared beliefs and values that foster social integration, a type of peer pressure by social class. That sure seemed to be the case here.

12: A Maternal Death

3/11/89: Susan just got back from a walk/talk around the neighborhood. She learned that a woman died last night giving birth. Very few births occur in institutions here, perhaps about ten percent. And the local institution is a maternity home staffed by an empirical midwife, one of the people Susan has been interviewing. The birthing woman died of hemorrhage. Also, another woman came in yesterday who had given birth nine days ago at home and then got the *susto* (a folk disease of fright) and came to the maternity home to be cured.

This week, Susan also interviewed a woman who had had nineteen births, two of which she delivered completely by herself – and then had her tubes tied. It is interesting that she refused to take or do anything to space births, yet she was willing to tie her tubes. At this very early stage of her research, Susan suspects that some women here don't make a distinction between abortion – ending a pregnancy – and birth control in the sense of averting a pregnancy.

Susan has also been reviewing prenatal records from the health post. Do you believe that one hundred percent of women say they breastfed their last child? Some say they did so for up to two years. That does not seem compatible with the high fertility here, since breastfeeding has a contraceptive effect by inhibiting ovulation. Also, all the women swear they don't touch alcohol.

13: Improvising Car Fuel

3/10/89: Since we own one of the few vehicles in Upper Calos, we have become a sort of local taxi. For the most part that is all right with us because it helps us meet people. They appreciate the favor and easily open up to us.

3/15/89: Fred has now driven in the dark from Santa Rosa to our house four or five times. We always have our hearts in our throats, but we always make it. We tend to go to Santa Rosa on Fridays to shop, pick up mail and give an English class to Dra. Enízia, the friend who has helped us so much in getting established, and some of her medical colleagues. We come back after dinner, and it gets dark here at six p.m. On one trip up from Santa Rosa, the car started to sputter when it was almost out of fuel. Fred stopped in a *bodega*, bought a bottle of the sugar-cane-based *cachaça* that the locals drink, poured it directly into the tank and off he went. It was enough to get him to the fuel station.

Today, a day at almost the vernal equinox, we looked out in the yard at noon, and there was virtually no shadow! At three degrees south of the equator, we have the sun almost directly overhead. It was really something. We get twelve hours of daylight and twelve hours of dark with very little variation over the year – dark at six p.m. and light at six a.m.

We have joined the local Catholic church. It is the biggest show in town. We go into town for the nine a.m. mass and usually receive an invitation to lunch, which is the main meal here, at someone's house. That is a good opportunity for more data collection. Sunday is therefore definitely a workday.

14: Palm Sunday Social

3/19/89: So much happens here. We continually witness events that reveal how people live and perceive life here. Today, Palm Sunday, we went to mass at the local church in our *sítio*. The priest only comes periodically to the local church, on special days, so people in our area don't go to mass every Sunday. With nothing but shoes for transportation, the six kilometers into town are a deterrent. It is a big deal when the priest comes to our *sítio* to say mass. But it seems it is a big deal mostly for women and children. Only six men were at the church, which was otherwise packed with children and their mothers.

One interesting note is that there was no sermon. When we are in town for mass at the main church, the priest typically gives a long sermon, not only for the townspeople but also for the *sítio* owners, who only come up to their *sítio* on Sundays or on holidays.

After the local mass, Susan invited two women to our place for a *cafezinho*, coffee and sweets. Thirty people – eight adults and twenty-two children – showed up! They were curious but very timid. We served coffee, cake, cookies and soft drinks. They didn't stay more than half an hour, and it was great for Susan, opening more contacts for her. Everyone was very polite. It was good for all to lose their curiosity about us, and small events like this help us blend into the community.

3/21/89: The sun crossed the equator at noon today, the first day of spring in the Northern Hemisphere. Our shadows were directly beneath us – actually, we had no shadow! Tomorrow we will see our shadows to the south of us for the first time in our lives.

Food here is excellent, except there isn't a very large selection of vegetables. The seafood in Fortaleza is tops. Bottled water is easy to get. We have lots of bugs in our area, but we are screening the house in and should have them well under control soon. Lots of noises at night emanate from animals cute and ugly. The trip from Fortaleza is hot and lasts about three hours, ending on our rough mountain road, which has gotten smoother in our minds with time, as we get used to it. The first time it was a shock.

We are keeping an extensive notebook of anecdotes. It is something to read. We have two, three or four things of interest to add every day. Today we had our third flat tire. Our spare tire has now been in three of the four tire locations on the car. We are replacing each tire with new inner tubes, so three down, one to go.

This is Holy Week, and down here it is time for another vacation. Vacations happen all the time! There is no school on Thursday, since there is no separation between church and state in the schools, where ninety-nine percent of the population is Catholic. It's very interesting to see the mix of church and state here. For example, children are taken out of class to go to confession, to make sure they fulfill their Easter Duty. The classes Fred teaches continue to be great fun. The kids seem excited and interested. In one night class, an older boy who had worked in the field all day fell asleep in a front-row desk. The other students started making fun of him, but Fred told them to be quiet, since the boy no doubt needed the sleep more than he needed to learn English. He slept through the entire class and smiled at Fred, maybe in thanks, as he left the room.

We are off to Santa Rosa tomorrow. We have four burros in the backyard tonight, about ten feet from the back door. They are accompanied by the distinctive aromas of the stable, though we can keep the scent out of the bedroom. We have grown to like it.

15: Trick or Treat

3/24/89: Today is Good Friday, and a surprise custom greeted us this morning. Children go out and trick-or-treat for their parents' breakfast, getting food in bags. So, here they have costumes at *Carnaval* time and trick-or-treating for Easter! We rushed down the hill to our local *bodega*. Alfredo and Naisa were just getting ready to leave for the day, but he opened and made a good sale. So far, pretty much only people we have already met have come by, but it's still early. We don't quite know what to expect. At least we won't get our windows soaped or trees papered.

Because of *Semana Santa* (Holy Week), everything is closed until Monday.

3/25/89: There is a "window-soaping"-type night here. Last night, people all over the Northeast hanged an effigy of Judas from a tree or lamp post. They put donated money in the pockets (the thirty pieces of silver) and go around the area and rob whatever is not tied down or inside, particularly chickens (because of the cock crowing three times). If anyone can "capture" the effigy, that person gets the money. The activity is for men only. It began last night at eleven p.m., and for some ended when the sun came up, only to be repeated tonight.

We brought everything in, but it turns out we were probably off limits anyway. We did contribute to Judas's pocket, so that was protection money, but also, as the saying here goes, "The ants know which leaves to bite." In other words, they only steal from friends so that no one will complain to the police. Besides, a permit is required to hang the effigy, so the police know who to go after first. The men fortify themselves with lots of *cachaça*, but except for about two hours of drum beating, all was quiet. We left a bag with five oranges in a lighted area, but they were still there in the morning.

We only had eleven people yesterday for trick-or-treat. We have lots of stuff left. Tomorrow is Easter, so we will go to nine a.m. mass. The whole town, at least all its women and children, will be there.

3/26/89: Today is Easter Sunday. We went to nine a.m. mass, but the seven a.m. mass was just getting out, so our mass was rescheduled to ten a.m.

We have a restaurant nearby, about half a kilometer away. It is right along the stream that flows through our *sítio*. It is only open for Saturday dinner and Sunday lunch. Service is very slow. But the food is good, and we try to eat out about once a week now. We had a plate of French fries for an appetizer, grilled beef and pork, a rice medley, potato salad, beans, *farofa* (manioc flour, not our favorite, but it is invariably served with meals), a big beer and mineral water – all for U.S. $4.09, including tip. The waiter was one of Fred's students at school, so service was exceptionally good, although it took a long while to get the food. It wasn't like we had a plane to catch, and the ambience was actually very nice.

We get to Santa Rosa on Fridays, for the English lessons we give to Dra. Enízia and her colleagues, so we go out for pizza afterwards.

An interruption – six kids just came up the hill to tell us that Judas is about to be cut down. He's up about twenty-five feet. A young boy cut Judas down from the tree, and the kids tore him apart. We may have misunderstood, but the money wasn't on

62

him. We sort of figured that would be the case. When he was all torn apart, they piled up his pieces and burned him!

And talk about a small world, on our walk back from the restaurant, two cars passed us. Both had people we know. We are always running into people we know, which rarely happened in D.C. We walked into a bank in Santa Rosa, and two people we know walked in. We ran into one of those same two people two more times the same day in other stores!

We have hired an eighteen-year-old to help take care of Romey. She's the sister of a woman Susan has become friends with through the church records office. (Susan is checking the baptismal records to get a count of the births in 1988.) The teenager starts Monday and will stay here Monday to Friday, meals and a bed, for NCz$10 a week. That's U.S. $6.54 a week, an above-average wage. The director of one of the private schools in the area earns $12.42 a month.

16: Making Hats – Who Benefits?

3/24/89: A recent magazine article showed the homes of the rich in São Paulo and then interviewed a day laborer who gets thirty-three *centavos* (twenty-two cents) a day and cannot afford even the lowest level of nutritious food – manioc flour. The disparity is unbelievable. We have an example in our neighborhood, where women make straw hats. Each hat takes two hours to make. The women get five *centavos* (3.2 cents) per hat. They sell them to a man who can get them to the local clothes factory, where the factory pays six *centavos* per hat. They then turn around and either sell the hats or ship them to São Paulo for twenty *centavos* or add features to the hat (and it doesn't take two hours per hat to add these features) and sell and ship them for fifty *centavos*. They are then sold for NCz$2 or $3 (U.S. $1.31 to $1.96).

The one factory here takes in as many as one hundred thousand hats per month! And to top it off, the women pay about three *centavos* for the raw material for each hat. To buy a kilo of beans, a woman must make fifteen to twenty hats, which represents thirty to forty hours of work. Beans are anywhere from thirty to forty *centavos* per kilo, more expensive if you want them pre-culled of sticks and pebbles. Beans are all the poor people around here eat and all they can afford to eat.

The cycle is even more complex than this. There are certainly more middlemen. This is a subject we hope to do a photo essay on while we're here, once we gather the whole story.

17: School Days

3/27/89: Fred taught class again today and took his football. The first question was, "Is that a baseball?" They had a fun time throwing the ball around during the break. The whole school watched as Fred threw passes to about twenty kids who patiently awaited their turn about thirty to sixty feet away. The classes are great, too, particularly the smaller one of nineteen. Fred can do much more, and they are the most interested of all the groups. Class size has a lot to do with that. The fifth-grade class has a thirty-five-year-old man attending every day. No one makes fun of him, treating him as any other student.

3/30/89: Yesterday Fred didn't have any teaching responsibilities, so he took a walk up the mountain. It is higher than it initially looks. He got up into the bean and corn fields but not beyond, which consists of untillable rocky stretches nearer the top. The view was beautiful.

We have had sunny days with cloudy afternoons and rainy evenings. It has gotten downright cold at night. We use both a sheet and a blanket, something we never used in Fortaleza. It looks like we have solved the bug problem with the mesh screen we have had put in all the windows; the gnats never wake us up at all now. The screens are a big improvement. We are very glad we brought the mesh screen with us.

We go to Santa Rosa tomorrow to shop and get mail. We try to go only on Fridays, since the trip is so tough on the car, and it is very hot down there. Tomorrow we need to go to fourteen places all over town, some places only for one item. You spend all your time just trying to keep up, and if you get everything you need on a trip to town, you are very lucky.

Fred just got back from class. A violent thunderstorm caused a tree to fall over three power lines that run up the valley. Classes were called off. This letter is written by candlelight.

4/03/89: Fred had two classes this morning; they are going better each time. In one class of forty-six students, only twenty-three have books. The others write everything in their notebooks. The seventh-grade class – only nineteen students – has students ranging in age from twelve to twenty-three. The students pass grades when they can and sometimes take several years to finally complete a grade. If you miss twenty-five classes, you automatically must repeat the grade. There is no stigma to repeating, thank goodness, or else everyone would be at home. One fortunate unforeseen consequence of Fred's teaching is that it has opened doors to many homes in the community for Susan's research. Almost everywhere Susan goes these days, people ask her if she is the wife of the English teacher. We always knew Fred would do well here when people in the U.S. would ask, "What is Fred going to do there?"

4/17/89: The teaching is fun, but class has been canceled many times for various reasons: a general strike; no electricity (Fred has a night class on Thursdays); Holy Week; confessions (twice); and festivals. The English classes only meet once a week, which is too few times to learn a language in the first place. It is just not serious enough. Maybe there is a basic assumption that nobody from here is going anywhere anyway, which rubs our equal-opportunity bones the wrong way. You don't know until you try, and the system isn't helping the students try. They are not given an opportunity to succeed. But the kids are great, though Fred sometimes doubts what value he is serving. That is always hard to measure, particularly when the academic part is so disjointed and therefore largely ineffectual, so you can't even validly measure what usually is measured.

4/26/89: The regular English teacher with whom Fred has been working, Professor Z., has over eight hundred students. He doesn't give written tests because he can't possibly correct them all. He and Fred gave six written exams yesterday, and it fell to Fred to correct them. We can't blame his co-teacher; he has to compromise the quality of his teaching by increasing the quantity of his students so he can earn enough money to support his family. The way he is forced to teach would never be accepted in the U.S., but he is average or above average here because at least he shows up and tries.

6/19/89: Now that we are receiving mail directly in Upper Calos, rather than at the home of Dra. Enízia, the clerk at the post office in Upper Calos said she would tell one of Fred's students if we had any mail waiting for us there, so we are all covered. Pretty efficient, actually.

18: Lights Out

3/31/89: It's nine thirty a.m. on the last day of March, and we still don't have electricity. The cause: The tree they hanged the Judas effigy from last week one week later got its revenge by falling on the wire! We probably won't have energy until noon or later, so we are going to have to cook our two frozen chickens. It is drizzling outside. The Portuguese word for this type of drizzle is *sereno*, the same as the word for serene. Nice.

4/01/89: We are still without electricity – almost forty-eight hours now. We had to cook our two chickens and sausage this morning because they would have gone bad if we had waited any longer. As it turns out, it was a good decision. We also went to the cow sale this morning, and at least they were able to keep the meat for Fred to pick up later... whenever.

Writing to you must be good luck; we just got our power back.

4/22/89: We have streetlights now! They were always there but never functioned. For the stretch of our "populated" *sítio*, we now have eight nice, bright lights. Last night the clouds rolled in under them, and it was a pretty sight.

19: Vital Statistics

4/01/89: Having computed all the registered births in Upper Calos in 1988 (many are not registered, and we don't know how many are not), Susan has the somber task today of computing how many of those who were born died as infants. We know of one family whose last six babies died within two months of birth. The mother received no prenatal care and no care after the births. The maternity center is a two-hour walk from her home. If Susan returns early, that may mean there weren't many deaths to count. Another explanation would be that people didn't register infant deaths. All of this is part of the research. We are off to Santa Rosa this afternoon.

The phone company has an office in Upper Calos. They suggested that we give our family the number there, in case of emergency. They will then send someone out to our house to tell us. It may be a one-day turnaround but certainly no more and probably less. All you have to say is, "Oo kazal amerekanu, oo pie-e shahmow" (the American couple, Dad called). The number is _____. We sometimes must wait for an hour or so for a line at the telephone office.

Susan is back. She said there were not many registered deaths. Unregistered births and deaths will be hard.

4/08/89: A lot of Susan's work in the last few weeks has been trying to find out how many births there in the municipality of Upper Calos in 1988. This is necessary for all sorts of rate calculations, the two most important for her work being the total fertility rate and the infant mortality rate. She has now exhausted all second-hand sources: the church records (baptisms are typically the number one source); the notary public (birth certificates have to be paid for, so many people don't get them); the maternity center (only sixty-nine births were recorded there in 1988); and the health post.

Susan has come out so far with four hundred six births, though she thinks the real figure is somewhere above six hundred (six hundred to eight hundred). To get an accurate count she will undertake a survey of a random sample of women. She and research assistants she will recruit will interview women in their homes.

Deaths are similarly under-registered since death certificates cost money. People see little use for them, given the person concerned is already dead. This is particularly the case for infants, who are called "angels" when they die before their first birthday. Last Sunday, we witnessed a funeral procession in Upper Calos town. It was for a seven-month-old baby – the same age as Romey. The casket was a cardboard box covered with green plastic (like a baggie) and filled with flowers, so that only the "angel's" face was showing. The procession was all young women; the mother was nineteen. The baby had died of what they call here "children's diseases," i.e., dehydration due to diarrhea. The experience was very touching and painfully sad.

20: A Different Sense of Privacy

4/01/89: Anyone coming from Fortaleza or Santa Rosa into Upper Calos town must come along the road that passes our driveway. In the absence of telephones, drop-by visits are the norm and can occur at any time. People generally announce their arrival by clapping their hands at a distance from the front door of the house to be visited. Inhabitants then come out of the house to have a conversation or to invite the guest in. If no one comes out, one should not approach the house. Of course, dogs are the infallible Third-World doorbells as well. Duque, the dog of our neighboring *moradores*, helps announce visitors. We have an iron gate at the bottom of our driveway that we close in the evening. A closed gate is another local signal that the people of the house are not receiving visitors. Insistent visitors will clang on the gates or just walk around the limited fencing on either side of the gate.

Now that we are established here, people often stop by. In order, the following people stopped by our house today: The head of an agronomy project here in Upper Calos, just returning from the capital, Brasilia; a nun who is the head of education for the entire area; the mayor's wife; and the largest landowners in the area. At six thirty p.m., as we were sitting down to dinner, a boy from the neighborhood (his family is quite poor) came and asked in the rain and dark if we could take his sister into town. (He had walked around the gate.) She was in labor and wanted to give birth at the maternity center. We took her, arrived at six fifty, and the baby was born at seven fifteen! When we think of Susan's eighteen-hour labor! Susan was able to witness the birth at the maternity center and was thrilled to be there. We go back tomorrow to bring the mother and newborn home.

4/03/89: Susan's work is going very well. Anthropology always has a slow start, because one has to allow time to get to know people (and for them to get to know you) before you start popping questions left and right. But now the time has come. Fred, Susan and Romey are well known around here now. We don't think there's anyone in the whole county of ten thousand five hundred who doesn't know of the American English teacher, anthropologist and blond baby. Through words and deeds, we have also won a lot of friends in the area. We believe we have been well accepted by the community. So now Susan has started to conduct more formal, directed, in-depth interviews of two to three hours with key informants. These are women with whom we have an established relationship who are willing to talk about their health. It's a lot of work, but also a lot of fun. She has conducted two formal interviews to date, with many informal interviews as well. Some fascinating data are coming out. One of the women, thirty-five years old with one child and wanting more, received with great interest the information that there is a fertile time of the month and also a way to measure when it occurs.

4/08/89: We bought a scale for the maternity center in town. They had no way of weighing newborns, so we bought the scale as a present to the town for all the help they have offered us. Susan spent the morning training people to use it. Birthweight is generally considered the best overall indicator of development and of maternal nutrition status during pregnancy, as well as the infant's chances for survival. In exchange for the present, the two

72

midwives who staff the local maternity center are going to collect information on each birth. That will be useful to Susan in her work. Previously, all the midwives did was write down the date and the mother's name – and sometimes they even forgot to write down anything at all. For those reasons it is impossible to get any information from their records. Now they will record answers to fourteen questions for each birth.

We have found that we have much more of a sense of privacy than is typical here. Everyone here is very considerate, though, now that they realize that we do some things differently. The way we first met one neighborhood boy was surprising. We looked up from what we were doing inside our house and found him staring at us through an open window. Fred yelled at him and scared him off. He now claps his hands from a respectable distance to announce his presence. If we don't come out of the house, he then, being somewhat insistent, comes to the door and knocks.

4/26/89: Everyday something happens. This evening, after Fred had put dinner on, we had to drive a woman who was having chest pains to Santa Rosa. She has a history of heart problems. We have become the bus, ambulance and all-terrain vehicle for the area.

6/07/89: We go to Santa Rosa tomorrow for a special trip, taking a pregnant woman for a prenatal check-up. Our car gets used for these types of trips all the time for all reasons… you name it!

21: What Bugs You?

4/03/89: It's about three p.m. The gnats have been bad today since there isn't much wind. The gnats don't bother you if you're moving, but if you are sitting, they buzz the ear like crazy. We have a fan oscillating around the room, but the gnats take shelter on the leeward side of the head. We heard some good news – that the gnat season will be over pretty soon. On the other hand, there's another season for another type of bug right after this one. The mosquitoes here are dumb and not aggressive, so they are little problem, but the gnats! And they bite, given time. They go away at night and on windy days. They come only two or three at a time, but that's all it takes. Surprisingly, the bites don't bother Fred much, nor Romey, but they're driving Susan batty.

We are making plans to go to Quito, Ecuador, in early to mid-May. One of Susan's fellowship sponsors holds an annual meeting of all the fellows in South America, and this year it is in Quito. One real plus is that to get there we must pass through Rio de Janeiro.

Tomorrow we go to Fortaleza for two days to do errands, change money and accomplish other tasks. With deteriorating roads, it is now a 3.5-hour drive. We haven't been there for over a month. The teenager who was helping us in the house is no longer with us. We were too strange to her; she was amazed at our daily routines, including when we used forks to eat and not just spoons, and she needed training in some basic household tasks. We have decided to look for help that can come in daily rather than sleeping in.

4/08/89: It is Sunday, and Susan is lying in a hammock on our front veranda, just outside our front door. She just finished two batches of laundry by hand. Teresa, the *moradora* on our land, comes Monday to Saturday to do laundry, but there's so much with all of Romey's diapers and changes of clothes. Plus, since we are in the rainy season here, things that do not get used often enough get mildew. We just discovered a whole bunch of clothes that we hadn't been using were full of mildew. They all have to be rewashed and hung out to dry. To boot, until the rainy season ends at the end of May, it is hard to get anything dry. When it rains, we have to move everything on the line to lines we have strung up on the covered veranda. With all the rain, some things stay on the line for three to four days before they get acceptably dry – not completely dry. So, since today is sunny, Susan wanted to take advantage of the good weather.

Whoops! It just started raining (after all that washing)! The sky can be sunny one minute and pouring rain the next.

4/10/89: The rain has been incessant, and the cold and flu seasons are well underway. Many of the students at Fred's school have been suffering, with the temperature at sixty-two to sixty-six degrees at night, and many people have no way to warm up. They certainly have no heaters. The dry season is still two more months away. There has been more rain than usual this season (as opposed to some years when they have no rain at all), and some of the bean crop is rotting.

4/13/89: Last night we had a good strong wind but no rain. The wind drowned out the night sounds. All three of us slept through the night for the best night's sleep we have had in a long while. One sound, of the mango fruit dropping from the heights

75

of the trees and splattering on the rock parking area, often keeps us up. The "dripping faucet" bird is still around. And the four a.m. rooster right outside our window still calls, although last night the wind kept the rooster indoors.

We rode to Lower Calos today. We think it may be too far for Susan to commute. She may narrow her study to Upper Calos. We will see.

Fred bought beef and pork today, 14 lbs. of meat for under $13. We are not yet used to buying meat that is still body temperature.

4/23/89: Fred walked into the kitchen barefoot and stepped on a three-inch frog. We chased him out with a broom. The rule here is: Wear shoes and don't look where you don't have to!

4/26/89: We had a spider the size of Fred's hand outside on the edge of the porch; it is now dead. Yesterday, Teresa found a three-foot snake under her bed. Snakes can't get under our beds, since ours are all solid cement down to the floor.

4/26/89: Fred was sitting at the dining room table, looking out of the front door onto the parking area when he saw a giant toad, a *cururu*, advancing across the stones toward the front door. It was as big around as a large pancake. Fred watched as it leaped its way toward the front door, climbed up onto the porch and then over the threshold into the main room, glaring at Fred all the while. It was clear that *cururu* was not going to leave on its own, so Fred went over to it, wedged his foot under its body and flung it back onto the parking stones with a vicious flick of his leg. The toad landed a good twenty-five feet out, turned and just glared right at Fred, finally getting out of the sun in another direction.

Fred also thwarted an invasion of ants recently. He woke up one morning to see the entire ceiling moving. He literally shook his head and looked again, finally focusing his eyes on a four-foot-wide ribbon of ants working its way in one window, up the wall, across the ceiling, through the entire house and out of the window on the far end. He decided to cut the flow off at its source. He grabbed the bug deterrent we have and squirted it outside the house at the base where the ribbon started. That cut off any more ants from getting into the house, and the ones already in the house just kept on marching out until they went out the window at the other end of the house. We are glad we were not in their way. Apparently, the rain drives all kinds of critters from their homes, and they have to seek better shelter elsewhere. We are told this will stop sometime in May or June. We now spray the bug deterrent around the base of the house on a regular basis.

Right now, every day we see a bird or bug we've never seen before. Our porch light is an insect collector's dream. We have succeeded by and large in securing the inside of our house. We fear that we will lose the inside again while we are away for three weeks and will have to win it back. Nature is quick to reclaim.

6/07/89: We have had a change in our animal visitors. A walking stick, a good six inches long, and an adolescent praying mantis camped on our walls for two days before they moved on. The drier weather has pushed the giant toads deeper into the valley where the water is running, much to our delight. The bugs are still here but not as bad. We are told that on June 21, when the sun will be as far away from here as it ever gets, the bugs are expected to leave. We still have our little frogs, which always hide in creative places, but they are easy to prod out of the house.

22: Election Time

4/08/89: The presidential election this year, in November, is the first direct election ever held here. Young people age sixteen and up and older non-literate citizens have the vote for the first time. Everyone is curious about how the vote will go. There are at least six legitimate candidates now. If the left were to show well, would the army step back in? How will the campaign be run by the different parties to appeal to the thirty percent or more of voters who are non-literate? Certainly, the non-literate voters are day-to-day practically wise, but they are nonetheless non-literate. The more we are here, the deeper the story gets.

23: Stage I Qualitative Research – Developing Key Informants

4/13/89: Susan is conducting an interview right now out on the far end of the veranda. They last two to three hours. She did one yesterday with a woman who had eighteen children, eight of whom survived. After the interviews, Susan spends another two to three hours writing up the data. The mix of fact, folklore and lack of knowledge is a study of its own. Although this particular woman works at the maternity center, her misconceptions are wide and varied.

4/24/89: Here a lot of women take a particular pill, called the "Pill of Mattus," for menstrual regulation. This is often a euphemism for trying to induce abortion. We don't know if it actually contains any abortifacient properties.

Susan's work is going very well. She is deep into the series of two-to-three-hour interviews with women about health, reproduction and related topics. It is interesting that most of the women do not know that there is a fertile time of the month. They receive no education along these lines. All they know are orals and tube tying – nothing else.

4/26/89: Susan conducted another long interview today. The woman had had thirteen births at home, with twelve infants surviving. She even has her own birthing chair in her house.

4/27/89: Susan is doing another interview now. The time is about two p.m., and the rain has just stopped. The rains are different now – softer but lasting longer. The gully washers we were having three to four weeks ago have subsided. The clouds still come in our window, though.

5/01/89: Susan's work is going well. She hates to leave it for a month as we travel to Ecuador, since she knows she will have to regain momentum when we get back. The in-depth interviews with sharecropping women about fertility, health and their lives in general are fun and fascinating. But it is slow work in that you have to build up a relationship with each woman before you can ask for the interview. If you don't have a relationship, the women will not tell you anything but superficial things in the interview. Each interview then takes another three hours to write up.

24: Car Trouble

4/17/89: We drove to a beach almost due north of us on the coast. We were taking a chance on losing our meat, as we had no power in the house when we headed out, but we had made up our minds to spend a day at the beach. Although the ride to the beach was very enjoyable, the town on the beach wasn't much. It had an inlet with houses all along the west side behind a boulevard, as well as fishing vessels and lobster boats. The town has great potential, but it was quite dirty. Across from the inlet were beautiful white dunes and palm trees, eight hundred to one thousand yards away, but there was no access. It was all very hot. The beaches of northern Brazil may just be too hot for us.

The trip home was something else, however. The car broke down twice on the return trip. The right front brake wore out and got to metal on metal, jamming the wheel and filling the car with a burning smell. We stopped at one of the mechanic shops that are pretty much everywhere along the road here; they no doubt have a steady clientele. Fred had them completely remove the brake, and we carried on to Santa Rosa using only the left brake, although the smell of the burning brake accompanied us all the way. We stopped at Dra. Enízia's house in Santa Rosa, and she offered to lend us her car, but we thought we could make it home fine. On the way home, just as we got onto the mountain slope, as Fred downshifted to second to keep up our speed, the gear shift came loose within the gearbox, floating every which way in his

81

hand. The car, stuck in third on a steep upslope, quickly lost power and died. We did not want to leave the car, and walking home was out of the question, so Fred backed down the long slope freewheel. When we got to a level spot, he was able to turn the engine back on, slowly release the clutch, and get the car to move in third gear. We drove back to Santa Rosa and right into a downpour. When it rains in Santa Rosa, the streets flood up to 1.5 feet at some intersections. Fred drove carefully all the way back to Dra. Enízia's house in third, unable to slow down, and with the car trying to die in the middle of every "lake." Romey loved it all. We made it and opted to hire a cab to take us home, making another forty-five-minute ride back through the "lakes." We had left home at eight a.m. and returned at six thirty p.m. It seemed like we had been gone a year.

The only good news was that the power was back on when we got home. We would have lost all the meat we had gotten the day before.

6/07/89: The muffler fell off the car Friday night on our way home from Santa Rosa. It was raining and dark. Fred pulled out his Swiss army knife and cut the rubber supports to free all the detritus. He put it all in the trunk and drove off sounding like a Sherman tank. We must have lost one small section of pipe and can't wire it up, so for several days everyone will know we're coming. We hope to get it fixed on Friday. The roads these cars have to try to survive are a challenge. Our teacher friend asked Fred if any roads are like this in the States. Fred replied that the only ones we have this bad are still in existence solely for historical purposes.

6/14/89: After a string of sunny days, we have clouds and a steadily falling drizzle, with cool temperatures and winds to make it even cooler. We've lit candles to keep the temperature up a bit in the house, making it cozy inside.

We went to Santa Rosa to get the muffler fixed, actually replaced, plus part of the exhaust replaced, as well as having some welding and a wheel alignment done. It was about forty-five minutes of work, and it cost $13.40.

It was dark when we made our way up the "mountain" and back home, and we came across something we did not expect. Rounding a curve, we came to a quick stop; someone had pulled numerous branches across the road. Fred backed up immediately about fifty yards, surveyed the roadblock and looked for a weak point. He revved the car and took off as fast as he could get it to go and crashed through the sticks. We have no clue what that was all about, but we figured it was just kids looking for something to do. If it had been anything serious, the branches would have been much larger and more numerous. No damage was done to our new muffler.

25: The Fruits of Labor

4/17/89: The owners of our *sítio* are Brazilian. The people of Upper Calos call the absentee landowners tourists. The owners' land lies mostly unused, a shame, but they get a percentage of the crops from those who do work it. One woman recently bought about twenty acres, no house, for $1,200, a sum no one locally can touch. The rich hold the land, hence the wealth. Everything is done with "their permission."

4/22/89: The postage stamps on this letter are part of President Sarney's plan for the Amazon. Everyone says the plan is all talk and no action. Some analysts say that the power brokers – the people with land – won't let the president do anything because the uncertain economy makes exploitation the only thing that keeps them rich. There really is no moderate way to get anything done here. The people in power have no desire or pressure to change anything, because the people not in power have no access to any power. This makes the open, direct election in November potentially very interesting because of the wider franchise for youth and non-literates. This will allow many who have been disenfranchised to have some say. There is freedom of the press and speech, but everyone knows that if the armed forces don't like the outcome, they could step in and push democratic progress back twenty years.

Military service, a vehicle for upward mobility in some countries, is also cut off from the poor, since it has height

requirements and dental minimums, both being indic
affected by the nutrition of poverty. No one here in Upper Calos
is very tall or has many teeth. Thus, poor populations are locked
out, and the army is virtually guaranteed to be made up of men
from the middle and upper classes, who are more likely to
support the status quo.

Brazil's is a peacetime army, but army units are stationed
throughout the cities and countryside. Santa Rosa, a sleepy town
of seventy thousand, has military police "towers" in strategic
spots throughout the town. That's in addition to the civilian
police. Interestingly, Brazil has never had a revolution like the
U.S. or many other countries in South America. Some say one is
needed.

4/24/89: Poor people here are really living on the edge. For
people who work at our house (laundress, occasional gardener,
handyman, and combination house cleaner and babysitter for
Romey) we pay each NCz$4 per day – about U.S. $2.00. And we
pay better than anyone in the area. Some people say we are crazy
to pay so much, but in conscience we can't pay the going wage,
which is $1 per day. To give more than $2 per day would make
people think we have money to throw away. This would invite a
lot of people to come to the door asking for money.

So, we add to the $2 salaries by providing food, medicine
and clothes to the people who work here. We give away pieces of
Romey's clothing as she outgrows them, mainly to the women
Susan interviews. They love the clothes. No matter what little
thing we give, it invariably becomes the nicest thing in their
baby's wardrobe. Romey is constantly growing out of things.
And the medicines we brought with us are likewise in constant
demand. Every day, someone comes to our door and asks for

help, reporting that a member of their family has the flu, or a baby has diarrhea. So, we are an over-the-counter drugstore, too.

You ask if people resent us. We would say no. We would almost like it better if they would resent us. But they are used to a concept here in Brazil that is known in anthropology as patron-client relations. In such a system, people rely on social ties to try to meet their needs. The example of salaries in kind is very apt. Instead of giving people a decent salary, you give them a pittance and then give them further income in kind – food, medicine, clothes, favors arranged for them and so on. Then, rather than thinking they are receiving a salary they have earned, they feel beholden to you and become your "client." You are their patron.

They even call you this in Portuguese (*patrão* for males and *patroa* for females). They then feel qualified to ask for your help in any critical situation, and you are pretty much expected to help out. In exchange they offer you allegiance, fidelity and services. Other people don't bother you that much because everyone is expected to seek out his own patron. The patron for the *moradores* is the landowner on whose land they live. But we are in what anthropology calls a "liminal" position. We are not landowners, but we are clearly not peasants. We rent, but we are not poor. So, we run the risk of attracting more "clients" than we can handle. We are sort of up for grabs. Already Susan is referred to as the *patroa* of Teresa, the *moradora* on our land – without Susan ever having stated such a claim. Right now, we have all the "clients" we can handle.

26: The Adventure of the *Ladrão*

4/23/89: Last night, a Saturday night without rain, was a night to remember. A neighboring *bodega* was featuring a musician, which attracted people – men only – from all over. One young man decided to try to break into our car.

The scene: It was about midnight, and we had been asleep since ten thirty. Fred heard shuffling footsteps. For a second, he thought it was fruit falling, but then the sound seemed too regular and became a regular pounding. He looked out of the slanting shutter, which only allows one to see about ten feet out at a very low angle. Our lights were on in front, but he saw nothing, so he opened the shutter, which didn't squeak. He looked again and all he could see was the hanging laundry on the veranda. Then he stood up on the bed and saw a person on the far side of the car beating on the window on the driver's side – in full light!

Fred, wearing only his underwear and with bare feet, hopped down off the bed, grabbed his flashlight and the baseball bat, removed the framed screen and jumped out of the window. Shining the flashlight on the perpetrator, Fred saw that the lad – we refer to him now as the "*ladrão*" (robber), though technically he was a would-be robber – was either drunk on *cachaça* or not very bright, because he ducked down in the light behind the car, thinking Fred wouldn't be able to see him. Fred sneaked up around the front of the car.

The *ladrão* was crouched behind the car, beneath the car window and didn't see Fred. Fred stood as tall as he could, which here can be imposing, and towered over him with the bat high in the air. Fred confused his Portuguese, saying something like, "What are you doing to our dining room?" The *ladrão* heard and then saw Fred and began to run to the shadows on the side of the house. Fred noticed a rock on the ground and realized that the lad had been hitting the car window with the rock, but the window had not yet broken. Fred stepped behind the car and saw the *ladrão* disappear in the shadow. Fred threw the bat sidearm, keeping it low like a lawnmower blade, to the spot where he thought the *ladrão* would be and heard a thud and loud groan. With the flashlight, Fred looked for the bat in the darkness and found it immediately, right where it had hit the *ladrão*. He knew he had hit his mark.

Fred found the *ladrão* lying with his head toward the wall of the house, feet out, lying on his left arm. He had to be drunk to be down for so long. He got up very slowly but saw Fred again and disappeared around the corner of the house. Fred followed. The young man obviously had not cased the house, because the fence trapped him. He crouched behind a bush, but he was caught like an elephant behind a bamboo tree. Scared to death, he pleaded with Fred to let him go and then decided to make a break. He darted out to Fred's right, and Fred easily reached out and poked him with the bat in the right shoulder just to let him know that he could have easily been clubbed again. Though the opportunity was there to stop him completely, Fred let him go, and off he went under the trees.

Today, word is out that Fred can recognize the *ladrão* if he sees him again, which is probably not true, but that's all right. Fred saw his face only in peripheral vision and noticed he had collar-length very straight hair. There are footprints and a dug-up area where he fell, and the rock is in place next to the car. Fred took several people on a tour of the site. Everyone says the *ladrão* won't be back, that he is too scared, and we have to agree. He was too inexperienced to carry off his escapade well. We figure he was after the car's radio.

Romey slept through the whole incident, and Susan woke up during it, wondering why Fred was going out of the window after an animal. Other than a window on the car that won't budge, no damage was done.

4/26/89: Word has traveled. We think the *ladrão* has been pegged. Apparently, the description Fred gave of his clothes and height helped the *bodega* owner, who was in charge of the party down the street, to peg him. It appears the *ladrão* returned to the party after his attempt, and one person noticed that he was walking funny. He is a seventeen-year-old who lives about three kilometers from our house. He's not a local neighborhood boy. We'll find out tomorrow what people suggest we do next. He should still have a bruise somewhere and should still be scared.

4/27/89: Another day, another episode! It turns out that the *ladrão* who tried to break into our car does not live as far away as we were led to believe. Now we are told that he lives on the outskirts of our neighborhood. Fred's description apparently traveled fast, as well as the news that Fred would recognize him if he saw him again. We've learned that the lad's mother went to the owner of the *bodega* and said her son is sitting at home crying because everyone thinks he is guilty. He's seventeen, above average height, has straight hair and was wearing the clothes Fred described. His brother said the backs of his legs were badly bruised.

His mother didn't deny his guilt but said that her son denied it. Everyone says he's lazy and won't work, and apparently a while back he tried to break into the very same *bodega* where he attended the festivities with the musician. To top it off, the lad has now disappeared! Whether to Santa Rosa or Lower Calos, no one knows. The community pressure here was intense. Fred has been fairly successful in fixing the car window at least partially, so the damage done was really to the lad himself. It is sort of a paradox that people are not surprised but are shocked at the same time. Fred is still proud of his prowess whirling the bat.

5/31/89: Our midnight intruder, the *ladrão*, apparently returned to the area after we had left on our trip, but he didn't come up this way at all. Now that we are back, who knows what he will do. He may leave again. We are sure that he will not come by our house again.

27: R & R in Quito

4/24/89: We are excited about our trip to Ecuador. We leave on Wednesday, May 3, for Fortaleza and then on to Rio, and on Saturday we fly to Quito for two weeks. We will be back on May 27. Our house will get a new coat of paint while we are gone.

5/29/89: We are back from Quito. It is fun to travel, but it's always good to come home. All of us were tired, and our newly painted house with all its faults was a welcome sight. We are at the tail end of our rainy season and are looking forward to July–September, when the weather is dry and relatively cool with no mosquitoes. We did have to win back part of our newly painted house from the frogs; about six had moved back in.

28: Community Solidarity

5/01/89: Today is Labor Day here, so we went down to the town cemetery. The municipal government had organized a communal work morning to clear the cemetery of weeds. Since we are in the rainy season here, things grow like crazy. The cemetery had become completely overrun in just three months. About two hundred people showed up, each with a hoe, which is the all-purpose instrument around here. They cleared the whole place in two hours and then went to a barbecue sponsored by the town. Fred took pictures of the whole affair.

29: Adjustments to the Research Design

5/31/89: Among the decisions made in consultation with fellowship advisors in Quito was that Susan should do the major part of her work here in Upper Calos and then conduct a more general survey in the other research town. We will <u>not</u> move to Lower Calos, as we had originally planned. It was agreed that since the qualitative research she is doing right now in Upper Calos is time-consuming and should not vary too much between the towns, we will stay here as we do the quantitative part – the actual fertility survey – in both towns. The quantitative survey will then be the comparative aspect. The quantitative surveys are essential, since Susan has determined that reliable data are not available through existing sources on the variables she wants to measure.

Susan will employ research assistants to help her conduct the surveys. If needs be, she can stay at our friend's house in Santa Rosa for a few days at a time when she does the survey work in Lower Calos, which we think will be near the end of the year. Susan is working on her sample design now and will begin working on her questionnaire in the next week or so. She hopes to begin the survey work here at some point in August. Right now, she is aiming for a sample of about three hundred twenty women in Upper Calos, divided between women from the town and from the *sítios* that comprise the rest of the municipality. She is in the process of recruiting four or five women to help her administer the quantitative survey. The plan is for each woman to do about seventy interviews over two or three months, whatever time it takes. Administering the survey is not something you can do all day every day, because then it becomes too routine.

That we will not be moving is a relief, because it is cooler and quieter here, and we didn't look forward to moving and having to develop new contacts and neighbors. It took us a month just to find where to buy chicken here.

The weather is changing; now it is cooler and much windier.

6/07/89: Things have been quiet here since we returned. We are glad we were able to fall back into the routine so quickly. The weather has certainly cooperated, with very little rain. Now our clothes dry in one day instead of the "almost dry" in three days that we had to accept during the rainy season. There is a little increase in temperature during the day, and the nights are much cooler. The night skies are even clearer now. Last night for the first time we were able to see the Big Dipper. The North Star is always lost over the northern horizon, but it was good to see an old reliable constellation again.

30: Put Me In, Coach

6/07/89: We have both started running, the weather being so good. Fred is also trying to get more involved in sports here – volleyball and soccer. He played volleyball for three hours on Saturday morning. The youths who were playing were sixteen to twenty-two years old. They asked Fred to be their coach. Then he played in a soccer game on Sunday. He thought it was going to be a pick-up game, but they were an organized youth team. He played two half-hour periods and then was dead. At the half, Fred asked how long the time-out would be, and his team members replied, "What time-out?" Fred didn't do badly. Being nine to ten inches taller than everybody didn't hurt. But little kids were dribbling rings around him (which he expected would happen) and kicking the ball a lot harder and farther than he could. He made one mistake, though, when he slid to stop a ball. What he thought was a sand and dirt field was actually tiny gravel, and he tore up the skin on his leg. He continued to play, but his leg carried a reminder of the day for a couple of weeks. Nonetheless, the exercise was welcome.

Susan stops and talks to lots of people as she runs. This lets her meet new people very informally, which helps set up future interviews. She creates quite a stir, we are sure, because the only people around here who run are the players on the serious soccer teams. We've found a good dirt road to run on that winds among corn and bean fields through a wide valley. Fred thinks it's the nicest place he has ever run, with clean air and mountain scenery. And everybody says hello.

6/19/89: We had a nice, quiet weekend, the only action being the first volleyball game of Fred's team against another team on Saturday evening. Two teams came up from Lower Calos. One was a women's handball team, which is basically basketball with soccer goals instead of baskets. The other was a men's volleyball team. All took place at the local community center, which boasts a pavilion for dances and a concrete court. The court is used primarily for "salon soccer," or "*fulbito*," as it is called here, which is small-scale soccer that uses a smaller, heavier ball and requires excellent foot and ball coordination. The court is used for handball and volleyball as well.

As a team, we had had two practices. We went over positions, the international rules, plays and so forth. All of this disappeared in the enthusiasm of the game, which increased because of the good-sized crowd. If the referees had been at all strict, neither team could have played. But as it was, the other team made a number of blatant errors that Fred had warned his team members not to do. We are glad some things were enforced. Fred had worked with the team on blocking and had good success there. His team won all three games and now has a return match in Lower Calos next Saturday night. Fred thinks one of the reasons he was chosen as the coach is because we have a car. Add team bus to the list of community services we provide!

31: Mid-year Status Report

6/18/89: We've been in Brazil for about six months now, and every day seems about four hours long. Romey will be ten months old on June 25. They call her "*lourinha*" (Blondie) here because of her hair. She has only had one illness since we arrived, a bout of diarrhea, and that was back in January, during our first month in Brazil. She absolutely thrives here. We must say that the people who thought we were crazy to take a four-month-old infant into the field were sure wrong.

Fred also loves it here. Besides teaching English, playing soccer and coaching volleyball, he does most of the cooking, which is a combination of camping-style resourcefulness and gourmet cooking. He comes up with some wild dishes. He has been studying Portuguese assiduously since our arrival and is now quite good. He should be fairly fluent by the time we go home, which will be sometime between March and June of next year.

Susan's work is going well. She is finishing up with the qualitative research and beginning work on the questionnaire for the quantitative part. The sample design is all worked out and is under review by some statisticians. She hopes to begin the quantitative survey in August. With a sample of some three hundred twenty women and the help of some research assistants, she hopes to get that part done within three months. Then the same type of survey will be done in the comparative town, Lower

Calos. She will hire a new group of local women from that town to help her do the second survey.

The main group Susan is working with are women of sharecropping families. They farm beans, corn, sugar cane and cassava. They buy rice to make the daily fare of rice and beans. This year's rainy season (January to June) was overly rainy, so most of the bean crop rotted, causing hunger in the dry season that is beginning now, in addition to the hunger of the rainy season. The women have lots of children. Breastfeeding is minimal, despite what women allege. And women don't have much knowledge about their bodies. Though Susan's dissertation topic deals mainly with fertility and its regulation, Susan is collecting all sorts of data related to menstruation, pregnancy, postpartum, breastfeeding and other areas of women's health. She is enjoying the work very much.

The Second Six Months – Hitting Full Stride
July–December 1989

32: School Trials

7/04/89: Students have the month of July off from school. Here the school year starts in February and ends in December, with July and January off. Fred is taking advantage of the hiatus to teach an intensive English course to twenty of the best of his three hundred students. The class is three times a week, two hours a day. They started yesterday.

7/07/89: If you have any maps of the U.S. around, please send them to us. The school here doesn't even have a globe. Actually, maps of any place would be welcome. We don't think the students here are able to learn much at all under these conditions.

Fred just finished his first week of intensive English class for students who show promise. He invited nineteen students to the class, and thirteen showed up. He is having a great time. One adult attended one class and expressed pleasure, "What a good teacher you are… completely different from Brazilian teachers in method." The whole education system is really a mess, with little or no teacher training; what is taught is taught by rote memorization. The students in this smaller class are responding and seem to be having fun – at least they are coming back! One saddening aspect is that Fred sees so much talent and intelligence in these students, many as smart as the gifted students he worked with in the States. Yet the education they receive here will take them nowhere; none are likely to have any opportunity to ever leave the fields. Brazil is wasting an incredible resource.

recent editorial opined on how poor education is here in , putting blame directly on the rich, portraying them as trying to keep the poor from realizing what a "beating" they are taking. One other thing we are starting to realize is that everything is politicized here. Apparently, the party in power is holding up some funds for education until just before the election, to solve the "What have you done for me lately" problem (not having done anything for anybody before!) and so influence the election.

7/13/89: Classes are still going very well. A hardcore group of seven shows up every time for the special class, complemented by several floaters. Some have already talked about continuing during the normal semester after the regular classes. We'll see. Fred likes the idea, but he wants to try to work within the existing structure still and see if he can get it to function better. He already has an idea that there's not much to be done with the way it's set up now, but it's what will be here when we leave. He also plans to sit in on some of the other teachers' classes to see if the methodology for all of them is similarly weak. There aren't discipline problems at all, certainly not as we have them in the States, so that's a positive base to start from. Individuals may be committed to education here, but the commitment doesn't translate into action. Unfortunately, individual efforts and best intentions are not enough.

7/18/89: We had an eventful morning, taking the *sítio* owners up on their invitation to lunch. Fred got quite sick a few nights ago; he had a fever of almost one hundred two. By evening he was semi-ambulatory. Susan taught Fred's class that morning. Two of the students get up at five thirty a.m. and walk to class, and we have no way to let the students know about a cancellation. Fred would feel awful if no one showed up to teach the class.

Susan then went back to town in the afternoon to give her periodic English class to the mayor's wife and to buy our weekly allotment of chickens. We get two complete chickens – everything but the feathers – for two dollars a chicken. We are starting to get used to buying warm meat.

Fred slept in a *rede* (hammock) the night he was sick, what with the fever and all. He didn't want to disturb Susan or Romey with his heat and restless movements. He was surprised how comfortable it was. Everyone sleeps in *redes* here.

8/07/89: It's a beautiful day today. Fred is going to continue the intensive English class, one Tuesday night for the morning students, and one Thursday morning for the night students. The school trucks will be able to bring the students into school, since the trucks are already coming into town anyway, so he won't have the problem of getting those students who live far out to the school.

8/29/89: Fred just returned from class. The night classes are so different from the day classes, since the day students don't spend the day working in the fields. The kids at night are exhausted.

10/03/89: There are no classes tonight because it is the last night of a novena before the feast day. There will be no school Thursday night because someone is reading the new constitution on television. This means we will miss three weeks of English classes for the night students. We wonder where the new constitution places education on its list of priorities.

10/19/89: Fred had his two special classes this week, the ones for invited students, and they went very well. He is not reminding anyone about the classes, so the numbers stay down, as a lot of students invited themselves, and it was hard to say no. He wants only a small group of regulars, which is what he is getting now. Fred enjoys these classes much more than the regular classes and may give up the regular classes at some point. He hasn't had a complete week of classes for four weeks. Something always interferes. Classes were canceled one night because it was the last night of a nine-day novena, another two days because one was the Day of the Child in all of Brazil, the other the Day of the Student. What better way to celebrate the Day of the Student than to have class, but no one here sees it that way.

Professor Z. is getting himself in trouble with the school, as his absences now outnumber his appearances. Fred told the director of the school today that he can't mentor Professor Z. if he doesn't show up. The people at the school agreed with Fred completely, that he had not signed on to be a substitute teacher, but rather a mentor. Professor Z. admittedly has a very heavy schedule teaching in three schools per day in Santa Rosa and Upper Calos. He is saying that the mayor refuses to pay for the fuel for his trips to Upper Calos. But students come all the way into town from the hinterlands to attend his math and science classes, and often he is either too tired or too busy to show up.

Sadly, Fred sees something like the same trait in most of the students, too. They want lots of grades in the grade book, but they don't want to take tests. There is maybe an underlying idea that what they are learning really doesn't do them any good anyway.

Susan's interviewers are an excellent counterexample. Pay people what they are worth, and they work very hard.

33: A Visit from Home

7/04/89: Fred's father recently wrote that he will be coming to visit in September. We are very much looking forward to the visit.

8/06/89: Fred's father is due to arrive here around September 10 to 12 for a three-week stay.

8/16/89: The weather has been beautiful. We did have rain yesterday and today, but we are hoping the skies clear tonight for the lunar eclipse – complete from about ten p.m. until two a.m.

8/20/89: Well, the weather is set, the bugs somewhat less dense, an itinerary planned, and the car is gassed and set to go. We look forward to the arrival of Fred's dad.

During Fred's father's visit, we will take a trip to Tianguá, a town in the Serra Grande, a higher plateau by half than where we are in Upper Calos. We did a pre-visit there. It's about two hours to the west of us – only one hour if the roads were better. The weather is very pleasant, and there's a nice hotel where we can stay. Rooms have a bathtub, and the hotel has a restaurant and pool. It costs U.S. $18 a night. Very unfortunately, no one was staying there when we visited, an indication of the economic state of the country. No one makes enough money to buy the goods and services because the prices rise so rapidly. We hope the hotel doesn't shut down before we get there with Fred's dad.

The trip took us south along the escarpment of the plateau, through a national park with grand waterfalls flowing over the escarpment and among some beautiful fields of sugar cane, corn, beans and palm. The whole area is much richer than where we live. The roads on the plateau, which are not federal roads, were excellent. Climate and the fact that the landlords live on the land in that area, as opposed to here, where we have almost one hundred percent absentee landlords, no doubt account for the difference. It was nice to see a part of Brazil that seems to work right, or at least better. Although we still observed poverty, everything seemed cleaner and more abundant. We then descended on a dirt road with some beautiful views of the hot and dry *sertão*.

The trip across the *sertão* was probably the best taste of the area that we've had: dirt and sand roads, fords across streams rather than bridges, little towns completely different from the towns we're used to seeing along the major highway between the two cities of Santa Rosa and Fortaleza. The isolation of these towns from the money that travels along the highway was evident. The birds were fabulous. So many types, five or six new ones to us. Animals were everywhere.

Because of time and heat, we took a pass at a number of photographic shots that would have been excellent. One was a family of eight, all walking in a straight line on a trail through the middle of large, green bean fields surrounded by palms. Everyone was carrying aluminum pots to get water. Another was a flock of sheep coming out of the golden sunset down a narrow dirt road lined by a scrub-wood fence. The dust they were throwing up added to the gold in the air. We hope similar scenes will be there when we return. That will likely be the case, since we got a sense of timelessness there.

8/20/89: Fred's father is due here soon for his three-week visit. The young women who work with us are trying to teach Romey to say grandpa in Portuguese (*Vovô*).

9/20/89: With Fred's father here, the letter writing has dropped off to minimal levels. Last weekend, we took a two-day trip to Tianguá, the municipality we had visited in late August in preparation for the visit. The temperature is even nicer there than in Upper Calos. We took some back roads to find a small hammock factory. We took a different direction from the first trip and visited a small town that had been founded by the Jesuits in the seventeenth century for the acculturation of the indigenous populations. It was by far the most charming town we have seen. The beautiful church just happened to be having the Saturday children's mass, so we joined in. The town had a beautiful series of parks, all clean as a whistle and nicely planted, with a spectacular view of the *sertão* below. The whole combination made us admire the Jesuits once more. Their methods of peaceably absorbing – at least in some instances – indigenous populations into Portuguese culture were certainly better than some of the other ways practiced by Portuguese entrepreneurs.

9/28/89: In the evenings, the four of us – Fred, Fred's father, Susan and Romey – all sit on a great rock in the front yard and watch the stars and the banana trees blowing in the wind. What a simple joy! We wait for the flatbed truck to pass that carries the night students to town for school. We wave to them as they go by. Romey loves this part of the day and has internalized the Brazilian wave, which is different from the American wave. She is thrilled when the students wave back. Later, before bed, we have our nightly family game of national rummy.

The schedule here is steady. Fred's father accompanied Fred to volleyball practice and took team photos. We went to the pastor's seventy-third birthday celebration and to the fifteenth birthday party of the niece of one of Susan's interviewers. The fifteenth birthday is a very special event in Brazil, a coming-of-age for girls as they approach womanhood. Tomorrow evening, we will go to a songfest commemorating the anniversary of the appearance of a famous Brazilian singer here in Upper Calos forty years ago. Talk about cultural memory! On Saturday, we will take part in a family celebration at a nearby *sítio*. Then, at our house that evening, we are holding the fifteenth birthday party of Vaneza, our interview coordinator. Next week should be calmer, before we take Fred's father back to Fortaleza the following Saturday.

34: More Car Troubles

7/05/89: We have had a week of great weather – highs of seventy-five and lows of sixty-five. With the car hitting so many potholes, one of the car's motor supports cracked about twelve inches into the bottom of the car. Two hours of soldering and welding in Santa Rosa cost $6.89. Fred and the chief mechanic have become great friends. He runs his shop like a vocational education school, with about twelve young men working as mechanics while he supervises and teaches. We are not sure how much the workers get paid, but it cannot be much. But they do get training in an occupation that will always be in demand in this area.

We go to Fortaleza tomorrow to exchange money.

7/07/89: The trip to Fortaleza was awful. We got on our way at seven a.m. The roads are in horrible shape, full of potholes. On one stretch of three kilometers, we couldn't go over ten kilometers per hour. Except to change money, the trip is not worth it.

8/05/89: The highways are literally falling apart. Part of a road collapsed recently in the state of Sergipe. It swallowed two buses and sixteen people. The time required to travel to Fortaleza has now doubled. For any trip from our house to anywhere else, there is no way to estimate how far one can go in a day, and there are few places to stop along the way for a restroom, restaurant or sleeping.

8/16/89: Back to the trip Fred took to Santa Rosa last night. He stopped at an all-night pharmacy to get aspirin after an aborted volleyball practice. When he got back in the car at eleven thirty p.m., it wouldn't start – something with the wheel lock not disengaging. He and the team members sat there and kept trying. He played with some ignition wires and bingo, the car started, but it sounded like ice breaking in a blender. He checked the oil. It was a bit low. Then who should come along but Professor Z., the teacher Fred is mentoring, returning from Upper Calos on his motorcycle. He took one of the team members to buy oil. Fred put the oil in but got no better result. Then Professor Z. went looking for a mechanic. Fred assumed this would cost a lot. It started raining hard. The mechanic arrived. He watched Fred start the car and then turned the key a fraction to the left, and the noise stopped. It turns out that the starter motor had kept running because the key stuck! And the mechanic didn't charge anything! Fred made it home through the clouds. The visibility was about two feet. He got home at one a.m.

We had a flat tire on Monday and got it fixed for $0.65. We have lots of car problems, but the only cost seems to be time. At least everyone is helpful, and the price is right. We long for smooth roads, though.

8/28/89: We pay a tax to use the federal highways. We pay once a month for a stamp that you put in the upper corner of the windshield. It appears that the first NCz$86 million collected was not even placed in a bank or interest-bearing bonds and has lost sixty percent of its value due to inflation. When the government implemented the tax, it had no plan, and it seems it still doesn't. People just see this sad situation as business as usual. At least the money comes from people who can more readily afford it and not from the poor, who don't have cars.

10/17/89: Believe it or not, it has just started to rain. Our neighbor said that it rains in October for the cashew trees. It seems like just one rain cloud, but we'll take anything. The dust on the roads is incredible, some even getting into the pipe leading into the gas tank. Fred cleans it out every time he gets fuel. The trunk is always dusty. The road is being widened, most of it in preparation for the asphalt to be laid at some point in the future. This has left a thick layer of dirt on the road, making it much smoother for a section of the trip, but it is so dry that the dust rolls up ten feet high behind the car at almost any speed. It is horrible for the houses along the road, and you really can't do anything for the pedestrians except a token symbolic slow-down and a wave to indicate that you at least tried to keep the dust down. The dust does not quit.

11/10/89: The car continues with more adventures, even since the last letter. In brief, another motor support cracked completely through and had to be welded. The new shock in the left rear broke one of its moorings at the top and was acting like a jackhammer on the rear shelf, putting a nice bulge in it; that was also welded this morning. The old weld (twice welded) broke on the exhaust pipe and had to be re-re-welded. One of the support hooks for the exhaust disappeared; the mechanic fashioned a new one out of something and attached it. And Fred just finished changing another flat tire, the second one this week. All for the cost of $8.01! All the repairs really cost is time, but when we resell the car, the value will be appreciably lower. The owner of the muffler shop said that we had better sell the car in Fortaleza, because everyone here knows all the troubles it has had and won't want to go near it. He also said that it has more welding on it than paint. Both are valid comments. We hope to laugh about all this when we get back home.

Fred had an interesting episode with Raimundo when they changed the last flat tire. The lug nuts were overly tight, as often happens when the prior flat tire has been changed at the garage, since the garage uses a machine to tighten the nuts. Both Fred and Raimundo, who is quite a bit stronger than Fred, tried to loosen the nuts with the lug wrench, but to no avail. To solve the problem, Fred found a stick about four feet in length and attached that to the lug wrench, giving his human effort added torque. Voilà! The lug nuts slipped off. Raimundo was astonished at this, a rare episode where we foreigners had an ingenious Archimedean solution. Those more typically are the handiwork of our neighbors.

11/11/89: More car news: On Fred's way to volleyball practice, the left rear shock repeated the same malfunction today, so, after spending five hours on Friday getting it "fixed," a return trip to the shop is necessary. That's probably why the repair was so cheap. And the tire Fred had fixed is leaking air from around the valve… right where he told the mechanic to look. We took two steps forward on Friday and two steps back today.

11/21/89: We had to buy a new battery for the car, and Fred had a flat this morning, but there is not much more to report. We make sure we park on a good slope so we can pop the clutch.

11/22/89: They have a saying here that follows "See you tomorrow!" It is "Se Deus quiser," or "God willing." Somewhat irreverently, Fred always retorts, "Se o carro quiser," or "Car willing." People laugh, so we guess it isn't too irreverent. And it's true. The car rules the house.

11/22/89: The car is fixed. It needed a new battery, which cost a month's wages if you are receiving the minimum salary. And the tires are all good, including the spare. It just doesn't get any better than this!

12/19/89: The road paving has not yet begun. We learned it is scheduled to start after this next rainy season, which has already started. We have had two days of inundation. But, thank goodness, no snakes have sought shelter in the house, even though Raimundo hasn't cleaned the roof yet. The steady mist was the source of a minor lake in the kitchen, but the rest of the house was fine.

12/29/89: Fred spent half a day today in Santa Rosa getting another motor support fixed. Believe it or not, three people asked yesterday and today what we are going to do with the car when we leave and how much we would want for it. We paid U.S. $3,583; if we get $1,000, we will be ecstatic. The supply of alcohol fuel is tightening, so the value of the car drops daily. Because the government sets prices, all gas stations here charge the same amount. We are not always in favor of free pricing, but that's what they need here to get the prices to a reasonable level for production and the consumer.

35: Money Troubles, Part Two

7/07/89: Here's an economic insight: The dollar is ahead of the curve of inflation, prices are a little behind it and wages are at the tail of the curve. For example, bottled water was twenty-seven *centavos* when we arrived. Yesterday we bought bottled water for seventy *centavos*, but the U.S. equivalent was even less for us – twenty-two *centavos*. But seventy *centavos* is half a day's wage for some of the workers here. For teachers, it is a day's wage.

7/26/89: The *Cruzado Novo* is now floating against the major currencies and has risen from 1.00 per dollar to 2.00 in about two months, but the unofficial rate is at 3.75. One example of how tough the inflation is on the local businesses here: The *bodega* owned by Alfredo's brother sold five cases of beer one weekend. When the brother went to replenish his supply of beer, the money he got from selling the five cases only got him four cases in return. He lost money on what he had thought was a great day.

8/03/89: The dollar had continued to get stronger while the prices were frozen. But in the last month and a half, now that the freeze is off, the dollar has slowed its climb while prices are skyrocketing. Still, our home energy bills since we've been here have only amounted to a total of just under $10.00. But now we're paying more than ever for propane gas. It appears that the authorities don't plan to do anything about the escalating prices until the election in November. The official dollar is up to around NCz$3.70 today, but that doesn't match the thirty percent inflation.

Our rent, which has not been raised since we moved in, has dropped from U.S. $67.57 to $31.25 per month. We think our rent has not been raised because we have maintained and made a number of improvements to the property, the screen "windows" being the most noticeable. All the dynamics and implications of the fluctuating economic situation here are an education to watch. People cannot believe we have had the George Washington one-dollar bill for so long. The government has just introduced a new NCz$200 bill that will hit circulation in November. People say that all Brazilians are learning to be economists.

8/06/89: Inflation has been hitting this country hard in the last months, and every month it increases. Inflation was twenty-nine percent for the month of July alone. There was a wage and price freeze during January to May, but now that it is off, prices are skyrocketing. People are afraid that the hyperinflation that hit Argentina is going to hit here, too. And we have seven more months of the government of José Sarney. Elections are not until November 15, and then the new president will not take office until March 15. We think there is very little hope of improvement until a new government comes into office. A lot of people are faring very badly, particularly those who must buy their rice and beans on the low wages earned around here.

10/03/89: The dollar hit NCz$9 yesterday. When Fred's father arrived, it was at $4. It has doubled! Everyone wants dollars, as the economy is on the verge of breakdown.

10/17/89: On Saturday, we went to buy meat and got over eighteen pounds for just over U.S. $10. We think the dollar is a bit ahead of the prices again.

12/12/89: The dollar was stable at about NCz$13.00 last week. Then it jumped to NCz$24.00 in one day yesterday! Today it has settled to NCz$20.00. With the second round of the presidential election this Sunday, it is anybody's guess what will happen to the dollar.

36: The *Quadrilha*

7/09/89: Sunday, drizzly, a nice day to lie low. Last night, Susan went out with other women to one of the local *sítios* for a *quadrilha*, a dance very similar to square dancing. Two groups performed, one made up of young children and the other of adults. The groups practice, but the performance certainly isn't polished, which makes it all the more charming. Susan and her friends walked to the event and back home, which was about a six-kilometer roundtrip. Walking here is fun and easy and particularly beautiful at night, with all the stars out. It is, though, a little spooky with the creaking and cracking of bamboo and the croaks of the frogs.

Two young women just dropped by who were at the *quadrilha*. They didn't get home until five a.m.! Only young people were left, all the *velhos* (old people) having called it a night. We have been going to bed as early as eight p.m. We guess we are *velhos*.

We had another two sets of visitors today, just as we were sitting down to lunch.

7/13/89: We have an amazingly windy day, like Chicago in the winter, only warmer. The sky has clouds whizzing by, with a bright sun dominating all. The praying mantis is back on our veranda. All in all, a nice day.

37: Volleyball Diaries

7/13/89: Fred took two softballs and two mitts with him, as well as the infamous bat, to try to show the volleyball team what baseball is like. He soon realized that it would have been wise to bring ten mitts, so each player could have one. As a result, the experiment fell flat. It was clear that *fulbito* and soccer do not teach hand-eye coordination. The young men were lousy at throwing and catching the ball, let alone hitting a pitched softball. If each had had his own mitt, that would have sustained interest and perhaps helped with catching the ball. As it was, the experiment died after one try. They all thought the sport was crazy anyway.

8/16/89: Yesterday, Fred taught classes in the morning, a one-on-one class with Professor Z. in the afternoon and another class in the evening. Then three members of the volleyball team and he traveled to join a practice of the university team in Santa Rosa. They drove for forty-five minutes through the rain and clouds. When they got there, they found out the practice wasn't happening. There's an expression here – *"Não deu jeito."* Loosely translated, it means "Things just didn't work out." It is the only excuse people seem to need, no specifics or further explanation required. But the team looked good making the effort and will be considered seriously for other events. They know they "owe" us. This type of "owing" works here. Perhaps that's what a Catholic country does. We have been invited for practice Saturday and games on Sunday. We will probably be roundly beaten, but who knows? The floor we will play on is wood, which is a luxury, compared to the hard concrete surface in Upper Calos.

8/20/89: Fred is in Santa Rosa today with the volleyball team, practicing against the university team there. He also went yesterday for several hours. He is busier than ever between volleyball coaching and teaching. In addition to his nine weekly classes, Fred is also continuing with the special advanced English classes, which meet once a week for two and a half hours. He has commitments virtually every day. We are constantly driving back and forth to the town of Upper Calos. The drive takes about twenty minutes – once the car is warmed up. The air at this altitude and the alcohol-run car don't agree, so getting going in the morning always takes some time.

10/01/89: Fred told the team the good news that they will soon be receiving new volleyballs and knee pads as a gift from his father. They were genuinely excited and are starting to feel like a real team. Their thanks were profuse. Supposedly, Lower Calos is coming to play tomorrow night, but no one believes they will show. And we have our new poles and net installed. The poles are permanently placed on the sides of the soccer court, which is great for volleyball, but Fred wonders whether some soccer players are going to break some toes and crack some skulls. A practice is scheduled for tomorrow morning if Fred can get to town, although many people will be going to mass and a funeral. Fred may cancel the practice or run it later.

10/03/89: The team from Lower Calos did show up Wednesday night, and we are proud to say that we won the first game we played with the balls that Fred's father bought. Before the game, Fred made a presentation to the team of the balls, with his father's compliments. The boys all cheered. They looked great in the new shirts and knee pads, and they played well in the first game. Fred thinks they got complacent once they had proven themselves, and the concentration wasn't there for the second game. He didn't play because he had to referee, his first time ever, but no complaints. Afterwards, some of the fans asked why he hadn't stolen the second game for our team! We were too bad for him even to consider doing that.

Fred told the mayor that his father had purchased the balls, and the mayor was very appreciative. No one here writes thank-you notes, but please realize that the team for the first time looks like a team and has the equipment of a team. The lads are very proud and love it.

10/19/89: The Upper Calos volleyball team, the Spikers, is doing very well at practice and at one set of games we had last weekend. They may be ready for some good competition. The guys love the knee pads but only wear them for games, so they never really have learned how to use them. This will make the pads last longer but won't help their volleyball game any. But they look good!

The team from Santa Rosa may come up here Saturday night for some games. We will get confirmation on that tomorrow. Fred goes to Santa Rosa tomorrow for fuel, water, food and other things, so he will find out if they are coming. They were supposed to come last Sunday, but they only got halfway here because they decided to rest at a bar along the way!

Another group of adults and adolescents has asked Fred to help them start up a team in one of the *sítios* way out in a far-flung part of the county. Too bad there isn't any money in this.

10/28/89: We are supposed to have a volleyball tournament today in Santa Rosa, but the man who is setting it up was supposed to get in touch yesterday to tell us the times and still hasn't done so. Our bet is it will be canceled.

It was to be a tournament of mixed teams, meaning a minimum of two women on the court. It seems that Fred started a family fight, which he bets was a good one, because the husband isn't friendly to him at all anymore. Here is the story: Fred discovered that a woman in Upper Calos town had six years of volleyball experience. But her husband wouldn't let her play with the team, even though he plays on soccer teams. She was furious and told Fred all about it. Perhaps the husband is insecure, and, the way men around here sometimes behave, he probably saw it as a threat. The woman now has a bit of shame about the whole matter, primarily because of her husband's attitude. It is too bad all around. The team could have used an experienced player.

We have four women, one who is very good and has some experience, but we have three who try hard but have no experience at all. This makes it difficult, because the men on the team don't like to play that much with the women anyway, and when the women make mistakes, the men get on them. Yesterday at practice, the four women showed up, and one of the men, admittedly the most immature of the group, suggested that the practice be just for the men. Fred told him that he was all wrong, that the tournament might be the next day and that we had called the practice precisely for the purpose of preparing for the tournament.

11/11/89: It's a good thing we went into town last night to double-check the volleyball scheduling; the game has been moved to tomorrow. You would think that in a non-telephone environment people would plan and make their plans well in advance, but we find that things are much more spontaneous than in the States. Maybe volatile would be a better word, as people are all last minute, but they have no way of letting you know.

11/13/89: The volleyball yesterday went very well, although Fred must remind the team constantly about positions and getting down and ready. We lost all three games but got one to 14–14 before we lost. We gave them a run. The other team has a large pool of talent from which to draw, Santa Rosa, and it shows. They have some excellent hitters and a good deal of height. Fred is the tallest on the Upper Calos team by a good four inches. He promised the team that the next time we would win one game.

38: The First Household Survey – Are You Kidnappers?

7/13/89: The goal of getting the research team in the field in August for the more extensive interviews is still in place. Susan is working on her questionnaire. She is up to one hundred items already. The interviews that she has been conducting so far are providing questions for the questionnaire, and she is seeing that the answers she is getting are starting to run similar courses, which means that not much new will be forthcoming. Although every woman has a unique situation with a set of problems all her own, patterns for the population as a whole have emerged, and new patterns are not surfacing. Susan will conduct a few more interviews but not very many more.

8/06/89: Susan is doing the final preparations for the quantitative phase of research – the random survey of three hundred twenty women. She has recruited a team of five interviewers. They are all local women whom she has gotten to know or who come well recommended by her friends. Requirements were an ability to read and write, experience giving birth, ability to dedicate afternoons to the work, and an appropriate interest and willingness to work. The recruits are four women from local *sítios* and one woman from the town of Upper Calos. The latter will do the survey work in Upper Calos town, where the houses are more imposing, and people are better off. The *sítio* women do not relate easily to the "city" women, and the mayor's house was one that was randomly drawn for a visit as part of the survey, which certainly would intimidate the rural women. The rural women have had very little formal education, three only through fourth grade, and one is now in eighth grade. She went back to school at age thirty-four after bearing six children.

One of the interviewers is Naisa, our broom-wielding neighbor with the *bodega*. Another is Sônia, a neighbor who lives a little bit down the road and whose husband operates a modest *bodega*, not as expansive as Naisa's place. A third woman is Antonina, who lives in a neighboring *sítio*. The fourth is Vanda, the woman who, now in eighth grade, has the most education of the rural women. She teaches third grade. Her *sítio* is closer to town. Maria Félix, the interviewer who will do the town interviews, is in a higher class of education.

The questionnaire has been reviewed by all the necessary parties and has gone to the printer. The copies should be ready this coming Saturday. The job of setting the correct sample size and planning out the random sample is pretty well accomplished. The methodology of a sample can make or break research. Susan has worked on this for months, so it is a relief to see it falling nicely into place. With the methodology established, the interviewing should be fairly straightforward.

Susan will begin training the interviewers on Monday, August 14, and hopes the interviews themselves can begin two days later. The interviewing should take two to three months, depending on how fast the team is able to go. She is picking the random sample of homes this week. Her den is full of hand-drawn maps and little slips of paper for the lottery of the random sample draw. She has met her August deadline.

8/16/89: The team is ready to hit the streets tomorrow. The training, conducted in the main room of our house, has run three

123

half-days and has been quite exciting for the women on the team. This is the first time they have ever done anything like this, plus they are receiving double the minimum salary. That is wonderful for them, since no one around here ever receives even the one minimum salary dictated by law. The women have the chance to earn some decent money, since Susan received a small amount in one fellowship for research assistants. All the other work around here that is "women's work" is extremely underpaid.

Though none of the interviewers has much formal education, Susan is banking on the "school of life" diploma. Vaneza, the young woman who works in our house and helps take care of Romey, will join the team in the afternoons to act as coordinator. She has helped with a lot of the clerical preparatory work. She is very clever and has a real knack for the work. Since she has not given birth, she will not administer any surveys. But she can keep track of which interviewer is where at any given time.

The questionnaire is long, about one hundred fifty questions, and will take at least forty minutes to administer. So that the results can be compared to larger, established surveys of Northeast Brazil, Brazil in general and worldwide, Susan had to incorporate many questions those surveys ask. She also included questions more relevant to the local area that derived from her qualitative research and key informants, who were the women who sat for the long interviews with her over the past months. Interviews with women in the random sample who have not given birth, however, will be much shorter, since there is no maternity history to detail. Since Susan hopes to do about fifty interviews per week, this part of the research should take about six or seven weeks.

The team will go out in the afternoons only, since women – including the interviewers themselves – are engaged in household tasks all morning. With the main meal being the midday meal and with the heat of the day, women usually undertake more sedentary tasks in the afternoons, such as making hats, mending clothes or culling beans. They are more likely to be receptive to participating in an interview during that time.

Susan needed detailed maps of each of the forty *sítios* selected in the lottery for the random sample, to make sure she either reaches all the homes in each selected *sítio* or has the count if the *sítio* is too large, in which case she draws a random sample from within the *sítio*. She did many of the maps herself, but for more distant *sítios* she recruited several of Fred's students to draw up initial maps she could use as guides. Everyone knows her already, as she drives, hikes, climbs or scrambles to these *sítios* to do the mapping or check the students' work. Each of the twenty "areas" of the municipality of Upper Calos is represented. Curiously, it seems almost all the *sítios* that came out of the random selection are ones that are hard to get to.

8/20/89: The work continues to go well. The team of six – Susan, the four local women and Vaneza – goes out every afternoon between one and five thirty, each time to a different part of the county. Each team member does two or three interviews. It is a tight fit in the car. Two women sit in the front seat in addition to Susan as driver, and three sit in the back. Actually, it is a very tight fit, and the group weighs the car down considerably, giving very little clearance between the car and the road. And none of the roads are paved.

The team is enjoying the work, and the women interviewed, to a person, expressed their satisfaction with the encounters, even with the very personal health questions. This is the first time many of the women interviewed have ever had anyone express an interest in their opinions and thoughts about anything. The last time someone from outside came through was during World War II, when the women were asked the full names and ages of their children, the eligible ones being taken for the war. Not surprisingly yet still amazingly, the collective memory is working, and many women have asked if the group is planning to take their sons to the war. What war, we ask?

By the end of this week, Susan hopes to be more than twenty percent done, which means probably one and a half months more for Upper Calos. She will still need the comparative data from Lower Calos, but she will consider how to crack that nut when this part is finished.

A serious problem has arisen. A wave of kidnappings of children – for sale, allegedly, to childless couples in the States and Europe – is occurring in Fortaleza, with rumors putting the happenings as close as Santa Rosa, so the group is also getting hit with the question, "Are you kidnappers?" This has caused Susan much distress and underscores the importance of making your way in the community before you start quantitative research. If we had not been well acquainted with people in some key spots and had not employed local rural women as fellow interviewers, this type of rumor would have shut all the doors on the work. Here is where Fred's teaching in the local school is helping enormously. Nearly all the *sítios* have at least one student in one of Fred's English classes. You never know how your efforts are going to pay off.

The interviewers were all nervous at first but are doing very well. They are so excited and enthused about doing something like this. That makes the work very rewarding.

9/14/89: Ever since Susan started the quantitative part of the survey on August 17, she has been running wild. The team goes out every afternoon to do the interviews. Every evening and morning she reviews the past day's work and prepares for that afternoon's work. The survey is going extremely well, but the work of some of the women requires fairly close supervision. Review of one questionnaire can take more than half an hour, and there will be three hundred twenty questionnaires in total. As of today, Susan is sixty questionnaires behind! This phase of the research should be over within a month.

9/21/89: Last night was a night to remember. At about five fifteen p.m., as the team of six was coming back from the afternoon's interviewing, the car overheated at a point about as far away from our house as possible. The team had been interviewing in one of the most remote *sítios* in the county. The overheating was a result of the hefty load of people the car was carrying over horrific roads at very slow speed. Often in situations like this, everyone except Susan gets out of the car and runs ahead, but this time they had not done so. It gets dark here at six p.m., so they knew they were in trouble.

As luck would have it, a flatbed truck carrying four workmen and a full load of coconuts came by. In rural areas, people typically stop when they see someone in trouble, as this driver did. The team asked for a lift. At first the driver refused because of his full load, but he soon relented – except the only space was on top of the coconuts. So, all six women climbed up and found places on top of the coconuts. They were all laughing and having a great time as they rode along, except for the branches that kept sweeping the top of the truck. Fortunately, they were going very slowly, so the branches did no damage. The truck let them off at the main road, and the team started to walk home. They were all telling stories and comparing this day to others, saying, "I think the day we went to _____ was worse," or "Remember when we had to _____."

127

Here luck intervened once again. The mayor happened along in his car and saw the group. He went to a house nearby and contracted with the owner of a truck to give the group a ride home. The team finally arrived home at seven p.m., just about the time that Fred and the husband of one of the team members were about to set out in search.

This morning, with Fred thinking he can fix the problem, having had to do similar repairs once before, we set out to walk to the abandoned car. Fred's father, seventy years old, had the idea that the car was only two kilometers away, so he came along, though we tried to talk him out of it. We took a shortcut through a steep pass over the hills, thereby saving the six kilometers more it would have taken by road. We arrived at the car two hours later, having covered about eight kilometers total. We all made it, Susan better than Fred or Fred's father; all the walking and jogging she has been doing paid off. The countryside was beautiful, and the walk, though arduous, was a wonderful way for Fred's father to see the land. He said later it was the type of walk that one says one would really like to take but never seems to do so.

It turned out that the car, having cooled off, was fine, though it was perilously close to the drop-off to a deep ravine. It had been the load and the slow pace that did the car in. We added water and off we went. Fred and his father are a little sore, but all is well. The team went back to the same place this afternoon to finish up the interviews. The adventure continues.

10/03/89: With the car in repair, Fred got to class this morning on the back of Professor Z.'s motorcycle, but Susan was reduced to walking all over. She walked to one interviewer's house and then to another's, a total of about ten or eleven kilometers. She was all red in the face, but she's determined to lose weight, and this is certainly a good way. She went out again in the afternoon and added at least another four kilometers. She's out walking now to meet with two interviewers to talk about the questionnaires. With the car down and the feast day (many people make a pilgrimage to a revered site), women would probably not be at home to interview in many houses anyway, so it was a good day to catch up on some things.

The stories of supposed kidnappings continue to hurt us. One woman who was recently approached for an interview claimed that we were kidnapping children, flying them to the States and making mincemeat of them for sale. Through much discussion, the interviewer was able to allay her fears. She countered that if we wanted to do that, it would be a lot cheaper for us to stay in the States and kidnap children there, as the airfare would far outweigh the profit made on the mincemeat. The woman thought this over and said that that made sense. It's hard to believe that she could recognize sense when she sees it. But the interviewer got the interview. Having local women as the interviewers is invaluable.

There's another story going around – thankfully, not about us – about a hairy leg – a disembodied limb – that's on its way here from Fortaleza. It is described as a *perna cabeluda*, that gets into your house and scares you. Susan casually mentioned it during several interviews and women all responded, "Oh, yes, it's on its way from Fortaleza."

10/17/89: It's a quiet and hot Tuesday afternoon. Susan is out on the interview trail again, this probably being the last week of them, with only some mopping up to do, which she can do by herself or with one of the interviewers if she needs help.

Susan is somewhat sated with this part of the research – having to explain the research so many times, dispel the kidnapping rumors, visit over four hundred houses and deal with car uncertainties. It's been tough. She is far behind in her letter writing and newspaper reading, the latter to keep up with current events in Brazil. We have newspapers from the end of August she still has to get to. But the end is near. We are going to Fortaleza for a long weekend, Friday to Monday, when she is done with the Upper Calos interviews. We will just relax at our favorite hotel. Although Susan needs to do the same research in Lower Calos, she will work with a second group of women local to Lower Calos whom she will recruit and train. She will then supervise them, but she will likely not do so many of the interviews herself. Lower Calos will be easier to cover because nearly all the houses are right in the town, and the surrounding countryside is flat, since Lower Calos is on the *sertão* and not here in the *serra*.

10/19/89: It's been happily busy here. Susan is on her last day of interviews, or so she thinks and hopes. The car hopes so, too! She is starting to see a lot of repeat information in the interviews, which is a sign that the sample is working and should be winding down.

Fred took the official photo of the interview team yesterday. The first one was with everyone outside the car. The second one was with everyone in the car, and we were shocked. We had never really looked at the car with the whole team in it – six women, some of stocky build. The rear tires were way up into the wheel well, even with the new shocks and springs Fred bought last week. Also, we have now had to re-weld two of the three motor mounts.

About an hour after the team left, Susan came back on foot. Fred's first words were, "Where is it?" The car was only about two miles out. The team had walked ahead another three miles or so to do the interviews anyway. They are truly a good group.

We walked to the car. A cable from the battery had gotten crimped under the battery support. That must have happened last week when we started having troubles, and it must have slowly burned through. Luckily, a fellow came by whom we know well. He had a bunch of tools, so we disconnected the battery, spliced the wire, and found some tubing to put around it until we got home to put the electrical tape around it. The car started right up. Fred is getting good at this!

The interviewing team stayed on the job. They were working in a remote *sítio*, and, rather than catching the school truck home, even not knowing if the car would get fixed or not, they decided to stay and finish the work in that *sítio* so they wouldn't have to go back another day, given the bad roads. They were prepared to walk home. Susan waited at the bottom of the hill from our house to see if they were on the truck with the students. When she didn't see them, she went out after them. They had already started walking. She got to them after about two miles of their trek home. Susan feels very good about what they have accomplished. The group loves the work. One interviewer was even in tears talking about the moment when the work will end.

10/19/89: We have discovered that, particularly in a different culture, what first appears as a cause of something later turns out to be much deeper and more involved. For example, we thought that it was men spreading the kidnapping rumors. We assumed that the men didn't want their wives interviewed or receiving any special information or treatment. Well, in at least one case, it turned out to be one of the interviewers herself, who likes to start rumors and blow things up, perhaps just to make life a little more exciting.

Early on, the interviewer reported that several women were quite upset about the interviews and were very afraid. She alleged

131

that a young man was spreading the rumor that we were here to kidnap children. She told all this to Susan. Susan confronted the young man, who denied it all, and said he was not at all bothered by the interviews. He was determined to find out who was spreading the rumors about him. The interviewer was not thinking about how this type of story could affect the interviews and her high-paying job. She had no concept of the way these types of things can destroy a selected population, stopping all cooperation. She was obviously communicating in a time-worn way of exaggeration and rumor that was all wrong for this situation. She has since been straightened out on this and doubtless has learned a lot about bigger things in life.

At the same time, some men have exhibited quite a bit of *machismo* over the interviews. They are very few, but it does bear noting. The other trait, that of people's propensity to spread stories – like the hairy leg – and exaggerate, has surfaced several times now and offers another way to look at things here. The only way to find these things out is to live here and learn.

We are learning to reserve judgment, which sometimes we don't do in the U.S. We have learned not to trust first impressions so much. What we are seeing and living here will for sure offer some interesting insights and contrasts into the life we lead in the U.S.

10/27/89: We have returned to our routine with a bang. More car problems, more walking, but the heavy part is over. Susan is now only going to be buried under paper for a while, tie up some loose ends and then on to Lower Calos to set up another interview team there. It could take two weeks to get a new team organized. The team here is having withdrawal pains and, surprisingly, not because of the loss of income. For one interviewer, for example, the work was one of the most challenging things she's done in years, and she sorely misses it.

11/05/89: Susan's ten-week survey ended for the most part on October 20, though she is still working on the loose ends, mostly revisiting houses where the woman to be interviewed was absent on the day or days of her original visits. She is also doing some preliminary analysis. But at least the whirlwind is over. While it worked out well, the undertaking was quite a drain. The team wound up visiting about five hundred houses all over the county. More houses than needed had been drawn in the random sample in case the refusal rate was high; that rate turned out to be very low, so the team wound up with an oversample. The car broke down four or five times, and we spent a lot on car repairs. It was a combination of bad – or non-existent – roads and too much weight in the car. We don't anticipate car problems like this in Lower Calos.

Susan points out that these are some of the reasons so much social science research has an urban bias. The challenges to rural research are considerable. She deliberately wanted to work with rural women because of that bias. So much research that purports to have a rural focus in essence is based on peri-urban or close-in rural communities. Upper Calos is indisputably authentically rural.

On this past trip to Fortaleza we bought several household gifts, which Susan plans to give away via raffle to women who participated in the survey. She hopes to hold the drawing on Saturday, November 18, if all the interviews are done by then. It will be fun to go and give the gifts to the women. They have so little that any of these modest gifts will seem wonderful to them. The gifts are things like pots, plates, tablecloths, thermos flasks for coffee and kitchen utensils. The team is looking forward to the raffle very much.

Next week, Susan will probably go down to Lower Calos to start things rolling for the second part of the survey. She hopes to get most of the work done in December and January, but the Christmas holiday will surely be a factor.

11/10/89: Susan is winding up the Upper Calos segment. She is out right now with one of the interviewers, completing some of the *sítios* where people weren't home for interviews during prior visits. She only has about five to ten more interviews to do to tie up all the loose ends of the Upper Calos sample. The lottery is next weekend, and we have many prizes to give out. All the women who gave interviews have a chance to win one of the prizes, and they are excited. The other day, Susan drove into one of the *sítios* to finish up some interviews, and the women of the *sítio* rushed up to see her, thinking she was bringing them prizes.

Fred is taking a picture of the prizes. They are things that we take for granted but that many of the people here have never had, like plastic containers to keep the rats and ants out of the beans and a flashlight with extra batteries. With the dark roads, people love flashlights but can't afford them, and everybody has to be out in the dark here. We were looking for presents that would be appropriate specifically for women. The interview team likes the presents, so we think we chose well. The public relations will help counter the still-circulating kidnapping rumors, too.

We go to Lower Calos next week to talk to the mayor there about the survey, so the whole exercise will start over. Lower Calos should be much easier, and the results of the survey will probably be different, so it is going to be fun to see how it develops.

11/21/89: Susan had her meeting with the vice mayor of Lower Calos, and all went well. This was the same man who grilled her in February when we had just arrived and she wasn't quite sure yet of the lay of the land. He even intimated back then that we were here for other purposes. Apparently, some foreigners posing as missionaries had to be thrown out of his county because they were actually geologists looking for gold. We were accused of that by one person here, too, though accused is too strong a word. Well, the mayor must have checked up on us and gotten good reports, because he was much friendlier. He arranged for some of the local women to be there to meet Susan, and they are now helping to recruit candidates for her to interview for the new team. This again shows the value of establishing yourself in the community before conducting research.

11/22/89: Yesterday was a nice day. The team delivered some of the prizes from the lottery to the women who sat for interviews. At the start, there were only fifteen prizes, but the interview team decided it would be better to have more modest but a greater quantity of prizes, since household goods are so scarce here. More women could be winners that way, too. For example, sets of two towels were made into two prizes of one towel each. The whole team went on the delivery trip, and the team member who had conducted each particular interview accompanied Susan to deliver the prize to each winning woman in her home. They did four such visits yesterday and hope to finish by Saturday.

The visits took the team out on the back roads again, but the effort was well worth it. One woman, who won a fairly large blue plastic basin, was in tears of joy. She is about sixty years old and has a forty-five-year-old son living with her who is mentally ill. Some days she goes without food. We are sure this was the first time that she had ever won anything. Both Susan and the interviewer were moved by her reaction. The other winners were equally ecstatic. One woman won four wooden chairs made in Upper Calos for $1.35 each, another a tablecloth. The women take great pleasure in such simple things. And Susan needed this

135

kind of response after the drudgery and problems of the interviews.

11/29/89: Susan has almost finished delivering the prizes. All went smoothly and continued to provide the team with some measure of satisfaction. She is glad that the interviews in rural Upper Calos are over. Fighting the ugly rumors wore her out. The only negative was the deep disappointment among those women in some *sítios* when they saw that they were not winners. It is sad to see how much they were counting on the modest prizes that were in play.

Susan went to Lower Calos for a meeting, and things went well, except the car ran out of gas on her way home. The gas gauge doesn't work, and there is a small leak at the top of the tank intake, so we don't fill it up all the way. We probably put so little in last time that it ran out before we anticipated. Our plan now is to stop at our gas station every time we pass it. Susan didn't get home until seven thirty p.m., which is well past dark. She got a ride to and from the gas station from kind unknown people who stopped to help.

It looks like Lower Calos is a go.

12/24/89: A few days ago, we drove to deliver one of the last lottery prizes to the most remote *sítio* in the municipality. The *sítio* is in the direction of where the car broke down the night that the team rode back on a truck full of coconuts, but it is even farther out on the edge of the hills, overlooking the *sertão*. The view is beautiful and picturesque, but the road there is very poor. The road actually disappears into a cow path, so we had to walk some to get there. The people who live there go four hours by burro down the side of the mountain to get to Santa Rosa. To get to Upper Calos town, they walk one hour to a point where they can hope to pick up a ride. If they have a health emergency, that is problematic. We made it out of there fairly well, but Fred suggested that we take the last prize to the post office and ask that someone deliver it to the one remaining *sítio*. The last *sítio* in question is not quite as remote, but it's off a much hillier road.

It's a good thing we heeded Fred's suggestion. That same night, at about eight thirty p.m., the mayor's brother and three other men came up to our house. Their car had gotten stuck on the road out of that *sítio*, and they had walked the four or five kilometers in the dark – pitch dark, with clouds covering the stars all the way – to our house. We gave them a lift the rest of the way into town. But already, after only a few days of rain, some roads are impassable. Someone in that same *sítio* died last year because the family couldn't get him out.

The trip along the winding, cobblestone road we drove up from Santa Rosa to Upper Calos took about 45 minutes. The *sertão* below is green in the rainy season and dusty brown in the dry season. Santa Rosa is off in the distance.

Houses of the various *sítios* dot the Upper Calos countryside. The fields of beans, corn and other crops are largely on the slopes. The main road from Santa Rosa peeks out in the lower left.

The cobblestone road up from Santa Rosa leads directly to the entrance to our house, between the two rocks on the right. The house itself is up an incline of about 30 yards. The road continues to Upper Calos town, some 6 kms. away, where the road ends.

The house we rented belonged to a local landowner who used it infrequently as a guest house for their main house. We loved the large veranda and the mango tree in the front yard; the top of the driveway afforded plenty of space for our car.

Raimundo was the *morador,* or caretaker, of the property we lived on. He likewise lived on the property in a small house with his wife, Teresa, and their daughter, Julia. Raimundo was an indispensable handyman, and he and his family were among our friends. The word *morador* in the agricultural sense means sharecropper who lives on the owner's land.

Our local *bodega* – convenience store and bar -- was right next to the entrance to our house. *Bodegas,* which dot the countryside, are known by their two entrances that facilitate foot traffic. Men congregate in the evenings and on Sundays. Alfredo, the owner, is in the doorway; Raimundo is seated on the left.

141

On our first Palm Sunday, Susan met several local women who had gone to mass in the little local church in our neighborhood. Mass there was infrequent, since it was not an established parish, so a priest came only periodically. After mass, eight women and twenty-two children came by our house for a visit.

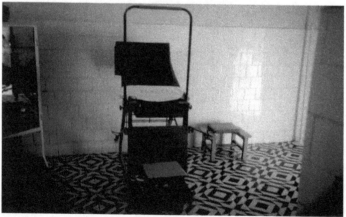

Two options for giving birth at the local maternity were a shortened bed and a birthing stool. In both options the midwife caught the baby as it was born. Many women gave birth at home, and some had a birthing stool of their own and acted as their own midwife.

The full interview team from Upper Calos posed for this portrait when we finished the training. From left: Vaneza, our coordinator, interviewers Sonia, Maria Felix, Antonina, Susan, Naisa and Vanda. Later Regina (not pictured) joined the team to help in data analysis. We would go out on weekday afternoons, after women had finished their morning chores and prepared the main meal of the day. Women typically spent the hot afternoons in sedentary activities, such as hat-making. This made them more receptive to an interview.

With Maria Felix conducting the interviews in town, the remaining six of us piled ourselves into the car – three in the front and three in the back – for the afternoon trip to the interview site of the day. The state of the roads off the main one and the weight of the occupants took a tremendous toll on the car. In all we had thirty-two flat tires, four motor mounts broken that required welding, two gas-line punctures, several exhaust repairs and replacements, and uncounted hours of unexpected walking.

When we had power, Fred periodically had to defrost the refrigerator. When the power was out, the refrigerator defrosted on its own, leaving a mess of water and meat that had to be cooked.

Romey made friends easily, and many neighborhood children would come to our house to play. Here Romey sits on our back stoop with Dona Maria José, a friend and key informant, and two of her children.

Virtually all women in Calos knew the art of weaving hats, a cottage industry they took up when other work was done. Women did the initial stage of the production and then sold their product to the first of several middlemen in a chain. Though extremely low paying, this activity was socially sanctioned and had the benefit of flexibility – and an opportunity to meet with other women.

July is coffee-picking season, the major income-earning opportunity for sharecropping families. Coffee beans were the major cash crop in Calos. Women and children picked the ripe coffee beans, running their hands down the branches as the beans fell into the basket tied around their waist. Even toddlers would help by picking up the beans that fell to the ground. Here two girls are at work.

A simple kitchen in a humble home. Poverty was the norm in Calos.

Our mechanic in Santa Rosa used the cars brought in for on-the-job training of local youth. We gave them lots of practice in fixing our car.

On the way home from one afternoon's interviews, the car overheated on a steep back road because of the weight it was carrying and the state of the road. The next morning Fred, Susan, Fred's father and Vaneza walked eight kms. to retrieve the car. This path was typical of the route we followed through the hills.

On Labor Day the town organized a communal work morning to clear the cemetery of the weeds that had overrun graves in the rainy season. About 200 people showed up, each with a hoe. They cleared the whole place in two hours and then went to a barbecue sponsored by the town.

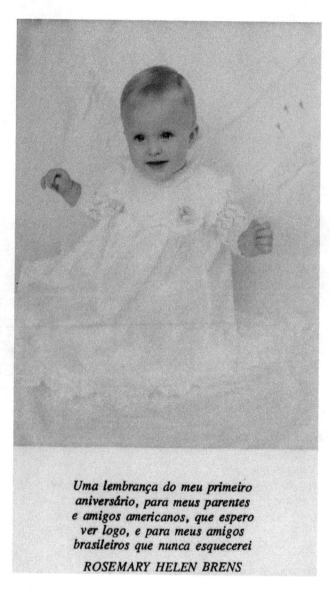

Uma lembrança do meu primeiro aniversário, para meus parentes e amigos americanos, que espero ver logo, e para meus amigos brasileiros que nunca esquecerei

ROSEMARY HELEN BRENS

Here is the commemorative card for Romey's first birthday, a significant one in Brazilian culture, since it implies the child will survive: *A souvenir of my first birthday, for my American relatives and friends, whom I hope to see soon, and for my Brazilian friends, whom I will never forget.*

The team met in the main room of our house to draw the lottery winners from among the 500 women who gave interviews in Upper Calos.

The lottery prizes were simple household items that many homes lacked.
Recipients were thrilled, as much with the notion that they won something, no
one ever having won anything before, as with the item itself.

Producing cassava flour *(farinha)*, a daily staple, was a family affair that involved several steps that took a day or more. Here a man wields the heavy hand-carved press that squeezes the juice from the plant before it is roasted.

Fruit was plentiful in our yard – mango, passion fruit, papaya, guava. Fred's father harvested his own bananas and papaya one morning.

154

During Fred's father's visit we hosted a 15th birthday party for Vaneza. The three young women who helped us with the house, the research and Romey pose at the party. From left: Rita, Regina and Vaneza.

We had simple but tasty dinners cooked by Fred. Here we are feasting on a chicken roasted in homemade barbecue sauce during the visit of Fred's father.

The road to Lower Calos began in Upper Calos town and wound down the opposite side of the hills from the road to Santa Rosa. Susan drove the Lower Calos road, a much rougher cobblestone road that snaked for 17 kms. along a narrower, more tortuous, less traveled and poorly maintained path, by herself on her many visits to supervise data collection in Lower Calos. Note the green *sertão* in the rainy season. The trip between our house and Lower Calos took an hour, more in the rain.

A team of four and Susan plus a coordinator conducted the 500 interviews in Lower Calos. From left: Ivanete, Fátima, Socorro (coordinator), Lêda and Aldenora. The team successfully completed the interviews in the outlying areas before the rainy season began.

In the long dry season the *sertão* turns brown, making it unsuitable for rain-fed agriculture. The vast arid plain is largely used for raising cattle.

Houses in the rural areas of the *sertão* tended to be quite humble. This household at least had some livestock.

To commemorate International Women's Day, the women of the community organized a procession. Many of the women sang a hymn. Some women were assigned to carry symbols of their lives as women. One carried beans and a hoe. Another carried a child in her arms. A third was the symbol of a widow. Still another carried a mop and bucket. Regina, on the left, represented the younger generation.

Berí's bar was just down the road. His wife, Sônia, started a business serving lunch, the main meal of the day. The place is still in operation today.

We took advantage of Sônia's wonderful cooking as a treat on Sundays

We loved the large mango tree in our front yard. When the mangoes were ripe, they dropped like pellets all day and all night long, often exploding on impact. Here local children are "harvesting" mangoes from our tree by throwing rocks up into the tree.

To clear the family *bodega* of rats, Alfredo went on the roof, removed the tiles and scared the rats out of the rafters. Naisa and the kids were below, waiting for the rats to drop and then batted them with brooms - - a family affair. On this day they got five rats, and the dogs ate two of them. Here is son Edmundo with his broom.

161

November is cashew season. Naisa taught Susan to clean the cashew plant by separating the nut from the fruit. The nut is the prized product, and often the cashew fruit is left to rot on the ground, to be eaten by wandering pigs. Some people make the fruit into a juice.

CONVITE

For our good-bye party we handmade invitations with the Brazilian flag and the American flag. We hand delivered about one hundred fifty invitations and thought maybe seventy-five people would show up. Over two hundred fifty people came! Our friends contributed a lot in kind with their help.

Susan and Romey at our good-bye party with interviewers from Lower Calos and their guests.

At our good-bye party Vanda, one of the interviewers from Upper Calos, makes a joke by pretending to trade drinks with her husband while neighbor Berí (standing) looks on.

This portrait of an elderly man and his dog reminds us of the gentleman who walked a long distance to our door to say good-bye.

We left Upper Calos in May 1990. On our veranda to see us off are, from left, neighbors Vanda (holding Romey), Maquel, Vaneza, Albênia, Rochelle, Regina, Julia, and Teresa.

Saying good-bye to Dra. Enízia

39: Where Coffee Comes From

7/13/89: Susan spent four mornings picking coffee about two weeks ago. She picked it on the *sítio* where we were invited to lunch that day in February. We are sure the landowner was taken aback when he heard she was out there picking his coffee. He lives in Fortaleza and has just come out for the holidays of July and stopped by with his wife to invite us for lunch.

We complimented them on the fact that the people who live on his *sítio* all have indoor outhouses (no running water). His wife replied, "Yes, we're trying to educate them." The patron–client relationship is a godfather–godchild relationship. All flows from above. The owners are nice but live a life very removed from the real needs of the people that depend on them and on whom they depend.

Unfortunately, the people here are so ingrained in the system of patron–client relations that they don't speak up for themselves much at all, and they wait for favors, the indoor hole in the floor being one example. And the reality is that these people are very bright. The kids Fred has in class are evidence of that. The economic class differences are tremendous.

Susan earned a total of NCz$2.00 for all her work picking coffee, equivalent to U.S. $0.63, enough for four soft drinks or eleven eggs. She gave her money to two of the women she worked most closely with. Ants were the biggest problem in the work itself. She still has about two hundred bites around her waist that only now, two weeks later, have started to fade and stop itching.

Performing work like picking coffee puts us in a desirable middle type of position. It allows Susan to float freely from one socio-economic level to the other very easily. People just think we are crazy Americans, not a threat. Establishing these relationships is a lot of work, and it takes much time. We have been here over six months, and only now is the ball really rolling.

Fred photographed all the people involved in the coffee-picking, taking about thirty shots. The coffee trees grow in the shade of old-growth trees, of which the landowners are very proud. The trees keep the coffee plants, some almost one hundred years old, from requiring irrigation.

40: All Politics are Local

7/20/89: The mayor is under fire from three re-elected *vereadores* (town councilmen) from the old regime, though not from the six newly elected *vereadores*. The gang of three traveled to Fortaleza to denounce the mayor to the governor, who happens to be of the same party as the mayor here. When the councilmen were asked the reason for their denunciation, they could not answer. In the old days, a simple denunciation was all that was needed to remove a mayor. It turns out that the mayor has not been giving the councilmen a cut of every monthly allotment received from Brasilia. That revenue is basically all the revenue the municipality has to run on, since the tax base is non-existent.

The mayor has beefed up the health post, providing a doctor every day, so people don't have to go to Santa Rosa. He also arranged to have three thousand coffee seedlings purchased for free distribution to the *moradores*. But without receiving a cut from the mayor, the *vereadores* don't have the wherewithal to give favors to their constituents. This upsets the patron–client relations. So, these three *vereadores* vote against anything that is good for the community if it uses money that they think they should be getting.

Well, the upshot is that the governor is sending someone to check the books, which the mayor is welcoming, but now the three disgruntled *vereadores* are trying to stop that, because the books from the prior administration are so bad. In one example, the new parts in municipal cars were replaced with used parts.

169

The group of three has started rumors that the mayor is bisexual and fooling around with all the women who work in his office. The mayor will hold a rally on Saturday night in town to open all this up. There will be a dance after the rally that will feature a singer from Rio. We will be going. As they say, all politics is local.

We are told that during the election campaign there was an assassination attempt on the mayor (then candidate). One very popular *vereador* was killed while he was driving the mayoral candidate's car and wearing almost the same clothes as the mayoral candidate. The candidate himself was in another vehicle. Three people were wounded, including one woman in the group that Susan picked coffee with. The attempt was made by the nephew of one of the other candidates at the order of one of the old retired *vereadores* who didn't like the mayoral candidate's ideas. Both are now in jail in Fortaleza, though for some reason the old man was released and came back here for almost a week before he was thrown back in. The current mayor has a good reputation and is doing a lot for the people, but people here are easily cowed.

7/22/89: The mayor's rally has been postponed until tomorrow night. Today, we went to the homes of some *moradores* who were processing manioc root into flour. Fred got some great pictures of people, the old wooden pressing tool and the large drying stove, which is eight feet across. Two or three families were involved to prepare sufficient flour for three months. The flour is typically used as a seasoning on beans and, as a last resort, as the only food during the hungry season. For the very poor it may be their only food. It takes an entire day to accomplish the task, but work is at a nice, relaxed pace, and the entire family shares the work. It was very enjoyable to watch and photograph.

We celebrated our sixteenth wedding anniversary yesterday. We are going to Santa Rosa for purchases, and then we will have pizza and fries for lunch to celebrate. Perfect, actually.

7/24/89: The mayor's address last night went very well, though it did not have the type of hype and staging that we're used to in the U.S. One could hardly see the mayor, the light was so poor, and people kept sitting in front of the speakers, causing the whine of feedback. But the mayor did well, holding up the book of expenditures at the end of the speech and inviting anyone to come any day of the week to take a look at the books. Nobody will or has the training to check the figures, but the symbolism was important. And word of mouth will get the news around fast. It was too dark to take pictures.

The event was one of the few times we have gone into town at night. The place was very lively, with the bars open and people in the street. There was Sunday-night mass, followed by the speech and a theatrical presentation and dance. We saw many people we know, many of them Fred's students. Unfortunately, the *cachaça* drinkers were tottering around in force, but it is amazing how people ignore them. They all know who the drinkers are – a simple gesture of an upturned thumb brought to the mouth when you're talking about someone tells all.

41: Less Power to You

7/24/89: We are in the midst of a *tempestad*, literally and figuratively a tempest! Winds have been blowing the rain almost horizontally. We've taken rain in the house where we've never gotten it before. As to be expected, the lights are out. Fred is typing this by candlelight on the computer, since we had to close all the window shutters. All in all, we haven't had any damage or problems. The storm is kind of a nice change.

Susan is out on home visits with one of the health post workers, tempest and all. Because of the deplorable home situations she encounters, she often comes back depressed from these visits, so we are having a nice warm pot roast (the beef is tough, so Fred has to boil it all day) and pasta meal. The lights just flickered, so there's hope, though the power has been off since early morning.

This is the last week of the special English class, with regular classes beginning next week.

7/26/89: The power came back on at six p.m. on Monday and then went out again sometime during the night. It didn't come back until Tuesday morning. Now it just went out again.

They are dynamiting across the street, where they have been building a hotel for the past three years. The hotel is owned by the brothers who own the *sítio* we are renting, but the financing is from the government. No one expects the hotel to be finished for three or four more years. It is huge. One wonders, why here and why so large? Tourism would be good for the area, though there is no organization for it, no sites set up or even sufficient

172

restaurants or facilities. Rumor has it that the hotel will be used for a government retreat and meeting place. It could supply some much-needed jobs if the pay is decent. They are putting in the swimming pool now, thus the dynamiting, when none of the rooms are even closed up to the weather.

10/27/89: Fred has dinner cooking. Susan has Romey out for an afternoon stroll. The power is still out, though Fred made a trip into Upper Calos town to tell the authorities that it was out. The last time the power went out the authorities were unaware, and we went almost twenty hours with no power. At any rate, Fred was assured that the power problem would be fixed today, but he is always prepared to cook the meats that are in the freezer.

10/28/89: Well, we have now been twenty-two hours without power. It's Saturday morning, and we don't need to defrost the refrigerator. The bad thing is that we have about ten days' worth of now partially unfrozen meat, so Fred will be cooking up a storm for the next few days, and we'll have leftovers from then on.

Fred is getting ready to go into town to talk to the power man. He spoke with him yesterday and was told that the repairman was in the field and would repair our problem when he returns. Fred asked if that meant today (Friday), and the power man replied, "*Tranquilo, tranquilo*" (Stay calm, stay calm). Well, Fred is going to find out exactly what *tranquilo* means, and if it means calm, he won't be. The whole *sítio* is out of power. Everyone here takes it as business as usual. That's why if you make a scene, you get a response, because no one makes a scene. They should fuss instead of putting up with this. We remember the lesson we learned when we first arrived in Fortaleza and were given that dark basement apartment in the back of the building. If we had not put up a fuss, we never would have been moved to the nicer apartment. *Quem não chora não mama.* The lack of respect shown the poor here is really a shame.

173

42: The Poor Get Poorer

7/30/89: Susan put in half a day today meeting with a woman in town and also trying to line up a job for one of the poorer women in our neighborhood. The job would be to make costumes for *Carnaval*. It looks promising, except it only pays NCz$0.30 per costume, about U.S. $0.095. At the most, one can make five costumes per day, for a total of NCz$1.50, but that's the same amount that you make picking coffee, which this woman, now five-months pregnant, does now. But she got drenched two days in a row last week and can't sleep at night because of the cold – all in all, not a good prenatal environment.

Wages are not keeping pace with any of the inflation. The baby food we buy has gone from NCz$3.60 to NCz$13.00 in two and a half months. Nobody here can afford to buy it; it would take coffee pickers eight and a half days just to buy one can. We go through two and a half cans a week. So, people here dilute the baby food to make it last, which unfortunately cuts a baby's nutrition intake and, if the water is not boiled, can cause diarrhea and dehydration, one of the major causes of infant death here. The fact that they do not take any photos of a baby until the baby reaches one year of age is very telling.

7/31/89: Susan came back from running this morning and said they were harvesting sugar cane along the road she runs on. Fred packed up his two cameras and the video camera and headed off. He took about twenty stills and a good bit of video that he will edit in the States.

43: More Critters

7/07/89: At one point today, Romey and Fred were looking out of our back door, and ten feet away were four cows, four chickens, two roosters, a pig, a big she-goat, a dog and two lizards. Romey really enjoys animals, so when she is riled up, we open the back door, and she settles right down. There are always plenty of animals to watch.

7/31/89: Another walking stick has perched on the screen we have in the main room. Last night, Fred got up to get a drink of water and almost stepped on a little frog right in the middle of the hall. The other night, a lizard ran across his feet in the dark and gave him a fright. He turned on the light and there it was, about ten inches long. He got a broom and gently guided the lizard to the back door. We don't even like to think about what goes on in our house after the lights are out. At least they let us have our peace in the bedroom at night.

8/29/89: Fred saw a fox the other night. No one likes them at all, as their only real prey is chickens. There are so few wild mammals here.

10/13/89: With the help of a book on South American birds that Susan's sister sent us, Fred has already identified twenty-three different birds. There are about ten hawks and lots of other birds that he is still identifying from among five to ten descriptions each. Our birdwatching is fairly casual. Fred sits in our main room and either sees something fly by or hears a new song. He is surprised to have that capacity – to be able to realize a song is new to the usual musical ambience. All serious birders surely have that ability to recognize songs, but it is new to him. We have never lived in such an open house, where all the sounds come in.

11/10/89: The other morning, Susan got out of bed and said, "I've never seen this type of insect before." Fred hopped out and there, on the corner of the mattress, was a scorpion. Thank goodness it was very small, only two or three inches, but it had its tail cocked for a shot at anything near it. Fred shook the sheet, and it fell to the floor, where Susan accurately and promptly put down her sandaled foot. No harm done, and we surprisingly were not that concerned, even afterwards. Fred figures it was a fluke, particularly since it was so small. It probably climbed in the open brick windows on the back wall of the house. It takes more and more to faze us.

11/11/89: On the local front, our neighboring *bodega* owners, Alfredo and Naisa, are clearing their *bodega* of rats again. While Alfredo is on the roof removing the tiles and scaring the rats out of the rafters, Naisa and the kids are below, waiting for the rats to drop and then batting them with brooms – a family affair. Susan recalls that killing rats was what Naisa was doing when she and Naisa met on our first day here. Today they got five rats, and the dogs ate two of them. At least the culprits are not the ugly rats one thinks of in the city; they are more like country mice. It was quite a sight to behold their youngest child, Edmundinho, who is about Romey's age of fifteen months, helping out by beating on already dead rats with a small stick.

11/13/89: We have a new pair of owls. One starts with a very long string of short hoots, and then the other comes in on a lower note, and they weave back and forth like that for a while and then move on to another tree.

12/12/89: Add "snake killer" to Fred's long list of achievements here in Brazil. We went to Upper Calos town for the largest festival that they have, December 8, Feast of the Immaculate Conception. Just as the procession was about to begin, a tremendous rainstorm hit. We happened to be on the road with a full carload of people and hit a puddle. The car died. We waited a couple of minutes and got help to push the car and were able to pop the clutch. Apparently, the rains happened on the day of the festival last year as well. We had five months of full sun and all of a sudden, with all the people on the roads walking to town in their best – and only good – clothes, the sky opened up. After ninety minutes of rain, everything went as planned, although many who had walked to town were soaked.

On our way home, the car died again at the bottom of the hill, so we left it there. We walked up to find two-inch ants crawling all over the parking area and the front porch; luckily, none were inside the house. The rain had driven them out of the soil. Fred went inside to get the bug killer to spray the door stoop so the ants wouldn't enter. As he opened the door to the storage room, a snake about two feet long fell to the floor in front of him. He let out a shout and then fairly calmly, according to Susan, told Susan it was a snake. He still can't figure out how he got over the snake to the other side of the room, but he did, grabbing one of the brooms in the corner. He smacked the snake roundly, but the broom broke. He continued to whack it while the broom broke down into five pieces. He grabbed another stick and shattered it, too. He then got the carving knife, stood on the body at the neck and cut the head off.

Research afterward revealed that the snake in question was a member of the coral snake family, medium-sized for this type of snake, highly poisonous and fatal if the bite isn't treated. The antidote is on hand in Upper Calos town. The snake was probably living on our roof, and the heavy rain forced it inside. This could only have happened in the ceiling-less kitchen area, so we are not concerned about running into a snake at night in bed. Besides, the snake had to work hard to climb the wall and get inside. We doubt there are others around our house. We will get the roof cleaned off next week, removing all the leaves and sticks, so we are fairly comfortable that such an episode will not happen again. But it was a rough ending to an already rough day. Fred kept meaning to take a photo of the snake. He had the snake in a large baggie, but it turned bad pretty quickly. Vaneza and Regina, another young woman from the neighborhood who works with us now, got tired of looking at it and threw it out.

12/19/89: Fred is watching a bird go after a moth out on the car right now. The problem for the bird is that the moth is inside the front window, and the bird is confused as to how to get to him. The moth is frightened, fluttering all around.

12/24/89: The other night, Susan walked out on the veranda right after a rain, and thousands of termites flew up out of dozens of holes in the front yard. The giant toads were all there in full force, surrounding the holes and eating what they could. The toads were in all sizes save medium and small! Fred got the Baygon and sprayed down the holes right next to the house that termites were emerging from and killed a lot of them. We don't need any more bugs in the house. The rains are bringing out all the critters.

44: No Signal

8/06/89: You asked about phone calls. It's hard to give a full picture of why it's so difficult for us to phone the U.S., but aside from the twenty-minute ride to the telephone office in town to place the call – which we gladly do – and the fact that we have to take a tired baby with us (because we phone in the evening and we are an hour ahead of the East Coast), the international lines are often busy, the operator from Upper Calos gets low priority on such requests (the international operator keeps putting us on hold), and the place we call from is always a zoo, because no one in Upper Calos has a phone at home, and there are only three public phones at the place.

We just got back from a day trip to a beach that *Sports Illustrated* has called one of the top beaches of the world. Well, the sand on the beach was way too hot, the water too hot, too salty and too rough. We have only been to the beach in the Northeast twice since our arrival, and we haven't been in the water more than two minutes.

Tomorrow will be a busy day for Susan. She is transporting three pregnant women to Santa Rosa for prenatal visits.

45: Presidential Elections Loom

8/20/89: We are heavy into the political season. On November 15, Brazil holds its first direct presidential election since the military coup in 1964. There are now eleven candidates. We enjoy following all of this because we have always been interested in politics.

The major problem is economic. Inflation is now running about thirty percent per month – over two hundred percent since January, even with a wage and price freeze in effect from January until early May. Every week when we go to Santa Rosa to shop, the prices have gone up a lot. Alcohol for the car goes up about every two weeks. Because we change money only periodically and inflation means the dollar keeps getting stronger, we are not hard hit, but the Brazilians sure are.

10/27/89: The dollar was at NCz$12.50 on Wednesday. It had been at NCz$11.60 on Tuesday. Who knows what it is today. That is an increase from NCz$4.80 in eight weeks. People are attributing the rise of the dollar to the success of the leftist candidates for president, as they are moving steadily upward, while the center-right candidate, Collor de Melo, who was at forty-six percent in the polls, has dropped to under thirty percent. The dollar is very popular with the rich, in case they have to leave the country, so right now everyone who can buy dollars is doing so, creating demand. As always, this is a problem for the poor, since it triggers more inflation, takes more money out of circulation and hurts productivity. Foreign banks don't even deal in Brazilian currency, so dollars are golden.

11/11/89: The presidential elections are this week. At the last minute, the current president, José Sarney, threw another candidate into the ring, persuading a television empresario to run. The empresario also has a popular TV show, so he is already well known. It appears that Sarney, who by law can only hold office for one term, was upset that another new candidate, Collor de Melo, who like Sarney is on the right but is critical of Sarney, had now climbed considerably in the polls and was now ahead. Sarney's daughter is running for office somewhere where Collor de Melo will probably win big and coattail Sarney's daughter's competitor into office. Though the television personality has only been in the race for ten days, he immediately jumped into second place, at eighteen percent.

This could have meant that there would be two right-wing candidates in the runoff election, rather than one from the right and one from the left. The empresario got his time on television during the electoral hour (each candidate gets as much time as he has seats in Congress – if the candidate's party has no seats, he gets eighteen seconds of airtime) and showed he had no experience. People fell for him because he is a television personality, sort of like running Johnny Carson for president (except Fred thinks Johnny Carson wouldn't be half bad). He was an obvious puppet for the decaying Sarney party. But thank goodness for the integrity of Brazil that the Board of Elections ruled that the empresario couldn't run. We enjoy following all the turns of events.

11/13/89: Wednesday is election day, coinciding with the one hundredth anniversary of Brazil as a republic. Everyone expects a peaceful election.

11/21/89: The elections here were very exciting. The counting lasted until Saturday morning, when candidate Lula da

181

Silva, the candidate from the left, received a large batch of rural votes and pulled ahead of another candidate and so qualified for the second vacancy for the December 15 runoff.

On election day, Fred went to Upper Calos town for volleyball practice, and the streets were packed. The trucks of the community were bringing people in to vote. It's obligatory to vote in Brazil, and the officials keep track. People know they must comply if they want a job in the public or the private sector. Everyone seemed pretty intense. Our car was filled going and coming. The municipality is divided into about thirty sectors, each with its own polling place in town, so there were lines all over. In spite of the obligatory nature of the vote, the country registered over nine million absentees. One report revealed that in a poor section of a major city people were afraid to leave their neighborhood and vote, for whatever reason. There were also over one million blank ballots and three million votes that were disqualified. Authorities said that next time they won't even count the blanks and nullified votes, since that slows the count down.

Some political analysts in the media point to the large number of blank and disqualified votes as evidence that the franchise is wasted on non-literates. Our sharecropper friends tell us a different story – that many people do this deliberately, in protest against the government. The thinking is that the government forces them to vote but does nothing for them. That is certainly a novel and probably accurate way to look at the phenomenon.

So, the runoff on December 15 will be Collor de Melo versus Lula da Silva, center-right versus left. This country desperately needs a change, and there are enough checks and balances in place to keep any program that Lula might introduce implemented at a reasonable pace. Collor would most likely change little, as he is the candidate of the businessmen in São Paulo, who put him up to run in the first place. Interestingly, Collor, new on the scene and a fresh face, forty-one, divorced, with a twenty-four-year-old second wife, received over seventy percent of his votes from the interior, where it was all image. Perhaps the voters lacked the sophistication to see that Collor is not offering anything. Even a little education hurts his chances: Only three students in the eighth grade support Collor. All the rest are for Lula, because they know that if nothing changes, they aren't going anywhere. People in the cities saw through Collor, giving him only twenty-four percent of their vote.

A combination of the left-wing candidates' votes totaled against the votes of Collor and the right would put Lula ahead by about four million votes, although there will probably be some slippage from the center-left candidates' votes. Lula is a much better speaker and really dwarfs Collor with his ideas and grasp of the problems of Brazil. The U.S. supports Collor and is ever fearful of anything with the connotation of the term "left." But the economic problems here are staggering and require someone in the government to put more value on people and country and less on individual profits. With all the profits of the empresarios going into dollars and then into Swiss and U.S. banks and not into salaries and productivity, the empresarios are afraid of Lula, who has already said he will put a stop to that. If he can get his ideas across in the interior, he can win by a lot. If he doesn't, he could lose, and Brazil will stay the same. If Lula is as smart as he seems, he will figure a way to win.

According to two sources of ours, some of Collor's people in Fortaleza have put money into the pockets of one of the local politicians, who then goes around to *bodegas*, talking the owners into putting up posters and voting for Collor. All of this will unfold in the next weeks. It will be exciting to witness it all.

11/22/89: Last night, the numbers were released from the first poll since the election. Collor has exactly fifty percent, and Lula has thirty-eight percent, with twelve percent undecided. We wonder if the polls are way off, since they conduct the polls by phone, which leaves out a fairly large portion of the population.

One person commented to us that with Collor in power, democracy would at least have a chance to settle, because his win would keep the military calm. Some people here believe that they have waited too long for change; too many others have given up that change can ever come. They certainly have no faith that it will come from the government.

12/14/89: A new poll last night put Collor at forty-six percent and Lula at forty-five percent. Collor is running such a negative campaign, even trotting out the first wife of Lula, who clearly still has some dislike of Lula, but she is not a political expert. Then yesterday the bomb dropped, when one of Collor's people quit the campaign because he alleged the campaign had given the ex-wife NCz$200,000 to talk against Lula. According to a friend who has recently come from Fortaleza, all over the city one can see Collor stickers on cars with Lula stickers plastered over them, indicating either people's switch of allegiance or some political handiwork. The last debate is tonight. Then no electioneering is allowed for the last three days before election day on Sunday. They call this "reflection time" in Brazil. That is not a bad idea in our view. All the football games have been moved to Saturday, so that no interference with voting arises on that account.

12/19/89: Election results: The election was very well run. Brazilians should certainly be proud of how well things went, after going twenty-nine years without a presidential election. Collor won with about fifty-two percent of the vote, and Lula had forty-eight percent. Lula continues as a Deputy in the House, and the left has a good number of members if not a majority. If Collor is smart, he can really do something here, but we fear he has no real push to change anything. We will see how things go. By the way, the dollar dropped to NCz$19.00 after the election result was announced.

46: Personhood for Romey

8/28/89: We celebrated Romey's first birthday and Fred's birthday on August 25 very quietly. Today, we shot forty-eight photos of Romey in different outfits. It is a tradition in Brazil to take a one-year birthday photo. Because of the high infant mortality in Brazil, first birthdays are commemorated more than births. As we saw early on in our stay, infants under one year of age are considered "angels." In anthropology we would say that personhood is conferred at the first birthday. We have chosen one of the photos to print up and make into cards with a little verse in Portuguese. We will send the cards out to family and friends. The backdrop is the blanket Fred's late mother gave us.

    11/05/89: We are enclosing here the commemorative card for Romey's first birthday. We are happy with how it turned out except that they spelled our last name wrong! We had forty made up and will be sending them out with letters to family and friends, plus we are giving a few out here in Brazil.

47: The Best Laid Plans...

10/01/89: The ride back from Fortaleza to take Fred's father to the airport was hot but uneventful. We made good time, as most of the road has been repaired. One section was bad, but, thank goodness, a bus was in front of us. Its weaving back and forth to avoid the holes forewarned us. When we got to Santa Rosa, however, to pick up more Xerox copies of the questionnaire and team shirts for the volleyball team, the man responsible wasn't home. We looked all over town for him but had no luck. So, Fred planned to go back down after dropping Susan and Romey off at home and out of the heat. Susan needed the copies of the questionnaire for the next day, and Fred needed the shirts for the volleyball game against Lower Calos. We went first to Vaneza's family's home, since she was keeping our house keys. The car died at her house. The carburetor or distributor is probably filthy. The mechanic will come tomorrow, we hope.

Susan walked back from Vaneza's home carrying Romey, and Fred stayed with the car to try to start it. Vaneza and her sister helped by carrying some things back to our house that needed refrigeration. Then someone came by in a truck and agreed to help Fred take all the rest of the things in the car back to our house.

Fred hit the hay for an hour to rest up for the volleyball game. He got up, dressed and started to walk to town. After two kilometers of walking, he got a ride on a truck that was carrying the drunken team that had just tied in a soccer game. He got to

187

town and found out that the other volleyball team hadn't shown up and wasn't going to! The fellows on the team had found that out yesterday but hadn't gotten word out to Fred. He started to walk back home but, fortunately, got a ride, since it is pitch dark here as of six forty-five p.m. With no questionnaires and no car, we will lie low tomorrow.

10/03/89: The car is still not functioning, but a mechanic, a young fellow from Upper Calos town, is at least looking at it. He removed the spark plugs, called *velas*, or candles, in Portuguese. He poured gas on them and lit them. Apparently, this is a way to clean them; an interesting method. We then pushed the car up and down the road to pop the clutch, but that didn't work. As this was happening, the battery died. The car should have started when we popped it, so we think the problem is in the carburetor, though the young mechanic seems to think that's still functioning. It is four p.m. now, and the mechanic has the battery back in town to charge it, so we're up in the air as to its fate. We shall see.

We cleaned out the shower head to get the water to run more smoothly, and now the heating element doesn't turn on. There is always something to troubleshoot. No wonder so little gets done in Brazil.

10/06/89: The car is fixed as of today. During the absence of the car, we both lost a good deal of weight and acquired some tan on our faces. Fred has five blisters on his feet from all the walking he did this week. He hitched several rides and even took a ride on the back of one of the trucks on his return from Santa Rosa. It was slooooow. He had to go to buy some parts for the car – which didn't solve the problem – pick up the team shirts, as the team was supposed to have a game that night with Lower Calos, for SURE this time, and Susan needed the questionnaires. We managed to stay afloat food-wise, since we had enough beans in the pantry. Susan, rather than continue with interviews, caught up on reviewing all the completed questionnaires she already had, so that was a big relief for her. Fred was able to keep all his commitments to the school, except for last night's class, but Professor Z. was going, so Fred could easily stay home. The problems with the car are too numerous to list, but they are all fixed, at least as of right now.

48: A Death in the Family

10/03/89: Raimundo, the handyman for our *sítio,* came to the house at noon today to let us know that his father had passed away this morning. They had been holding a watch at his father's house. His father was over eighty years old, though no one knows his exact age for sure, and had extensive heart and lung problems. He was never officially married to his common-law wife, although they lived as man and wife for a long, long time, so there is worry that his widow may not continue to receive the little retirement money that they have been getting, which is about $15 per month. The wake, called a vigil, is tonight and the burial tomorrow morning, on the Feast of St. Francis. Because of the holiday there is no school. In its place will be major religious celebrations in the morning and the evening.

We will not attend the wake this evening if the car is not fixed, since the walk is too much, particularly at night and with Romey. The vigil goes on all night.

49: Entrepreneurial Spirit

10/19/89: We are glad Susan has found some good, intense people. We are going to take one woman in particular to a hammock factory that is set up in a town about sixty kilometers away. The woman is very interested in getting a home factory started up in her *sítio* here. She is also the one who asked Fred to help with the volleyball team and is even politically informed, which is very rare here. This woman is very active in the liberation theology movement as well.

It appears that many people don't have an idea of political right versus left, conservative or progressive, but are swayed by looks, with not much understanding of the issues. Many have expressed interest in one particular candidate who espouses positions that are against their interests, but he looks good on television and the posters. It is hard to expect much political savvy when there hasn't been a general presidential election here in decades.

Except for the woman interested in the hammock factory and a handful of others, we are not finding people with a lot of intensity, perhaps for good reason, as it doesn't get you many places. Some people who have shown it have been assassinated, particularly those in the economic and agrarian reform areas. The people here are open, friendly and wonderful, but it is a problem for the people themselves that they are not going to bring about the changes that are needed. It seems that someone is going to have to do it for them. The situation is not very promising, but it is ingrained in the patron–client nature of the culture, and that is hard to root out. It will be interesting to read the letters from us that Fred's father has saved and see how our views change the longer we are here.

11/13/89: We made the trip again to the town with the hammock factory. The name of the town has now been changed. The owner of the land asked that the town be named after him, and he isn't even dead yet! The egotism causes all kinds of confusion, since the placards on buses, road signs and maps of the state will all need to be changed. The woman we took with us has been very interested in starting a hammock industry here in Upper Calos. We saw the factory itself. It has four big manual weaving machines that require substantial coordination to use. Fred asked the owner's son if he knew how to work one of the units. He said no, that it was too much work!

We also visited three homes where they had smaller machines that make a panel one-third the size of the hammock. They then sew the panels together. The whole family gets involved in this cottage industry. They do the whole process: dying the thread, spooling it, weaving it and sewing it, right there in the house. They provide a finished product to the factory owner, who then takes it along with his hammocks to the stores he has established as his market. We hope to return and videotape the whole process.

In one home, the husband makes the single-panel looms. We bought one for the woman with us. The cost was about $18 for a fairly complicated piece of machinery. But, since it is all wood and strings, the material is inexpensive. The cost isn't much to spend to get a cottage industry started. Our budding entrepreneur wants first to make hammocks for everyone in her *sítio* who doesn't already have one; many poor people sleep on the floor.

Then she hopes to produce for market. We counseled her that she will need to sell some hammocks to resupply herself with thread.

One home had a crucifix on the wall, which is not at all unusual, but on one side of the cross was a painting of a white girl and on the other of a white boy, each with blonde hair and the big blue eyes that were popular in the Big Eye paintings of the 1950s. The two children running around the house were beautiful kids with deep brown eyes and dark hair and skin, but the cultural message of the self-concept that these paintings represented was crystal clear and very sad to consider.

50: Time is Relative

10/17/89: Without anyone telling us, we lost an hour of time over the weekend. The philosophical question arises – Can you lose an hour of time if you don't realize you've lost it? It is because of the "Schedule of the Summer," or the Brazilian version of our Daylight Savings Time, only no one here in Upper Calos goes by that schedule, but just down the mountain, Santa Rosa and Lower Calos do follow it. This, of course, causes great confusion. People here go with the diurnal rhythms, invention of clocks or not. Fred went to watch a football match that was being broadcast on TV on Sunday but was wondering why he missed the first half.

We really do live outside of a time-structured environment. Even Susan's requirement to meet people at specific times is not very stringent. She had a meeting at one p.m. at one of the *sítios* to allay fears anyone might have regarding the interviews. When she got there, no one was there. Like the volleyball practices, slowly and then more rapidly people started to show up, and before you know it, the place had thirty-five to forty people inside plus lots outside looking in the windows. Having the car show up in the *sítio* was the signal that the meeting was forthcoming. Who needs time?

51: Where Cashews Come From

10/17/89: It turns out that the trees we thought were cashew trees aren't. They are some other fruit. The cashews are now starting to come into town, fruit and nuts, the ripe ones seemingly coming from higher up in the hills. We have some small fruit but nothing near maturation yet.

11/13/89: On Saturday, we had our first good rain in months, since May. It was very pleasant and cooled everything off. We had a rainbow, too. Fred is shooting video of the cashew, which is coming in now in droves. Cashew is quite a weird fruit.

11/29/89: Susan has been out two days this week picking cashew fruit. People don't like the fruit, so they wait until it rots and then pick it off the ground for the nuts. Some feed the fruit to the pigs. Naisa roasted some cashews the other day and gave us a portion. They were delicious!

52: Meat from the Source

11/13/89: Fred attended a cow carving almost from the beginning last Saturday. The carving started so early that it was still dark. It was a real lesson in biology. And for the first time, since we were first in line, we got the filet. The filet is much more tender than the parts we usually get, which is why it's hard to get. Fred picked up our two chickens and a big pork leg on Sunday. Now if the power stays on, we'll have meat to last a while.

11/30/89: We bought ten pounds of pork leg and ribs for fifty-six cents a pound. We are having more pork and chicken than beef. Both are cheaper, easier to cook and more tender.

53: Planting Season

11/22/89: Yesterday was also a day for fires, as farmers were burning the fields up on the top of the mountain behind us, using the age-old slash-and-burn technique to prepare the fields for planting. The crackle of the fire was background noise all day. The smoke filled the air, and the ash drifted in, particularly in the ceiling-less kitchen.

11/29/89: Fred just returned from filming the burning of our neighbor Alfredo's field. The field hasn't been planted for eight years. It took fifteen days to clear the brush. Some of it was twelve to fifteen feet high. They throw the brush onto the field as fuel for the fire. Flames reached thirty feet. It seemed well controlled, but we had news of another fire that crawled over a mountaintop and destroyed several cashew trees. Alfredo and his family will plant corn, beans and manioc. That will take another three to five days, all just in time for the beginning of the rainy season.

12/29/89: The roads have dirt washed out across the path in five or six places, but today we have some sun, so the storm may have been a fluke. The rainy season typically starts in mid-January. Raimundo certainly hopes the heavy rain was a fluke, since he hasn't burned his field yet, being busy with other jobs. We've given him NCz$1,000 to fix the refrigerator in his *bodega*, which he recently started up – the patron–client thing again, but he's a good man, and if U.S. $50 gets him up and running, the gift is worth it.

54: People

10/19/89: This is the last week of work with us for Rita, the other young woman who helps with Romey and the house. She is Vaneza's sister. Rita is pregnant and due in mid-November. She is having a hard time getting around. The walk up our drive knocks her out. We offered her half-pay for ten weeks, while Vaneza takes over. Regina, another young woman who has also done chores in the house, will continue as well. Regina primarily does laundry in the morning, as she teaches in the afternoon. Teresa no longer works inside our house. Regina will be earning more in four half-days of work here than she does in a whole month of teaching at the school.

11/13/89: We're going to Upper Calos town tonight. Fred volunteered to be on the judging panel for the art show that is part of Municipality Day. There will be a dance afterward. We find it hard to believe that they have these festivals on school nights. School attendance always suffers the next day.

11/22/89: People here are warm and friendly, though not necessarily polite in our terms. But you never really take offense because they are so friendly. And no one gets angry, except for the mean drinkers. Fred got angry with the students one day, and they have behaved perfectly ever since. They behave better for him than for other teachers. It's amazing how fast people respond. No one likes confrontation. They may be fearful of the violence that some confrontations generate. Fred was in one *sítio* that had a little cross alongside the road. He asked what had happened, thinking it must have been a traffic death, but that was not the case. A man had been killed in a knife fight at that spot.

11/29/89: On Sunday, when several landowners were in Upper Calos, they gathered at a neighboring *bodega*. A large table had been set up for them in a shaded outdoor area, and about six landowners were seated, with a few chairs empty. Fred was passing by, so they invited him to join them for a beer. It appears they had invited their male *moradores* to join the festivities as well, with the alarming difference that the *moradores* were not invited to sit. They were standing around the table, back from their hosts. From time to time, a landowner would pass a cup of beer back to one of the men. The *moradores* had what Fred saw as forced smiles on their faces, and Fred found the whole situation a bizarre yet clear indication of the stratified class relations of Upper Calos.

55: Friendly Competition Continues

11/30/89: We played our fiftieth game of national rummy two weeks ago. We play a game every night that we are home. Susan won twenty-two games, and Fred won twenty-eight. We are now starting our second round of fifty, and Susan is way ahead after ten games, but the tournament is still young.

The planets are very bright, particularly Venus. Fred is getting a bit better with the constellations. He knows the stars pretty well in our home latitude in the northern hemisphere, but everything looks different here near the equator. It is still hot here in the afternoon and really hot in Santa Rosa and Lower Calos all day long. We are very glad we live up here in Upper Calos.

56: Christmas in Fortaleza

12/23/89: We had planned to go to Salvador da Bahia for Christmas, but the state of Bahia was receiving so much rain that roads were washing out even in the state's capital, the city of Salvador da Bahia itself. There is flooding throughout the state. We decided to spend the holiday in Fortaleza, and we are there now. It's raining here today, too, with humidity at about two hundred percent! But we have air conditioning at the hotel and a television with good movies. The shower, with hot and cold faucets, is a dream. We'll probably stay here until December 29.

12/27/89: We escaped the rains of Upper Calos to encounter the rains of Fortaleza. We have had only one partial day of sun since we arrived. We spent Christmas very quietly and quite nicely here in the hotel. Thank goodness for the extensive hotel veranda, which allows us to walk outside during the rain.

12/29/89: As of today, we have been in Brazil for one full year! It seems like yesterday and like ten years ago. We are back in Upper Calos, as Salvador washed out, and Fortaleza was wet, too. But we missed all the happenings here, where it rained for four straight days. Apparently, our handyman Raimundo was up on the roof even during the rain, repairing the roof to prevent drips. The walls show many water marks. The stucco is porous, and rain will penetrate but usually not leak in. The water marks are evidence that it really poured here. Upper Calos town was cut off for a day and a half because the bridge below the big water run washed out. The support did not wash out, so the bridge has

201

now been fixed enough for one lane to pass through. In addition to the rain, two earth tremors on the afternoon of December 27 rocked things up a bit. We missed it all.

We are glad to have sent all these long letters. They will help remind us of everything we have experienced here. It has been quite an experience, one that will certainly inform our perspectives for the rest of our lives. And why shouldn't it?

12/31/89: This is no doubt the last time that we will write this year. It's eight p.m., and the year is coming to an end. We plan to play some cards (the second set of fifty national rummy games is going slowly) and try to stay up until nine thirty or ten p.m. We will celebrate the arrival of the New Year a little early or in the morning.

The rains have stopped, and we have had sun the last two days, with only a hint of dark clouds. Everyone says that winter hasn't started early (winter only means rain here), that the rain in December was just a fluke. The serious rain will begin in mid-January. As of December 21, the sun has been traveling back north in the sky. We have a beautiful evening, about seventy degrees and dry. The clouds are gone, and a sliver of moon, Venus and the stars are out, with a cricket working the limited audience for all he's worth.

The Last Five Months – Very Much at Home

January–May 1990

57: The Last Stretch

1/01/90: Happy New Year! We made it until eleven p.m. before we crashed. Thanks so much for sending us the fly swatter. It probably has an effectiveness of eighty-five percent, taking into account the miscalculations of the wielder. It's quieter than newspaper. The cows go down to the *sertão* tomorrow and should take most of the flies with them. The fly swatter works on beetles, too, and for the past three days we've been having a hatch of them. The problem is that when you step on them, they let out a substance that appears to stain. They are leaving similar marks on the screens. A really filthy June bug is what they are. Even the giant toads don't eat them, though the ants might.

Fred went for a short jog today. His knees have had a good rest, and it felt good.

2/05/90: Rita, the young woman who used to work in our house, had a baby boy on December 1. Everything went well; she had the baby at the local maternity center, with a midwife attending. She never came back here to work because she has her own baby to care for now. Since Rita's maternity leave, her sister, Vaneza, has been helping us with Romey and the house. Regina, the other young woman who works for us on a daily basis, is twenty-two. She washes clothes in the morning, helps with Romey and then assists Susan in the afternoon with analysis of data from Upper Calos.

58: The Second Household Survey – Beating the Rainy Season

1/01/90: It's amazingly quiet today. Only two cars have passed by all day on the road below our house. Susan starts tomorrow in Lower Calos. Her team is recruited and trained, the copies of the questionnaire got done in time and the car is running well. Even if there is a complete lack of alcohol fuel, the vice mayor said not to worry, that he would have a driver come up and get Susan in the gas-engine car of the mayor! Everything should go much more easily in Lower Calos. The roads are better, and most people live in the town itself, so little time will be spent visiting *sítios*. When work in the *sítios* is completed, the team can walk to the houses in Lower Calos town, so Susan won't have to make the trip every day. She will go for supervision and quality control. She goes over every completed questionnaire with each of the interviewers. Susan is so thorough and so aware of her methodology requirements that these data will be useful to other people as well. She is very tired out, but the result of her thoroughness will be a level of excellence that will become evident in her dissertation and any other products that come out of it.

Our time here continues to be an education, and nature is still providing new twists. By February 15, the date we arrived here in 1989, we will have seen all the seasons that Upper Calos has to offer and, we hope, not have any more surprises.

1/03/90: Susan did not get to see the end of her first day's work yesterday because a brake went bad on the car. She is doing the rural areas selected in the random sample for interviews first, before the rains destroy the roads. The roads on the *sertão* are never as bad as they are here in the highlands, but even at that, last week Susan had to ford three streams that didn't exist in December. She got the interviewers out to their areas but had to come right back to seek repairs. She arranged a taxi to pick up the interviewers at an appointed time after their work. Driving gingerly at twenty kilometers per hour, she made it to our regular mechanic in Santa Rosa by five p.m. He replaced the brake for about $3.50 in labor, and the brake itself, the shoe, was $17.50. Susan didn't have enough money with her, so it was all on verbal credit, nothing written or anything. She will pay the garage today. She was home by six thirty p.m. last evening and will find out today how yesterday went.

It is now evening. Susan arrived home from Lower Calos at about four thirty p.m. today. It tends to be a bad sign when she comes home early. Nothing was wrong with the car, but the taxi driver with whom she had arranged a pick-up for the interviewers never showed up yesterday. The team was stranded ten kilometers outside town. They waited until six p.m. and then walked home. They didn't get home until nine p.m. Susan handled it perfectly today, listening to the whole story from the group and then giving them the day off with pay. The taxi driver had been friendly and full of smiles, so Susan thought that all would go well.

It is hard to see how this part of Brazil can get ahead when some people here have such a scant sense of responsibility. In another example, a woman whom Susan had hired as a local coordinator was supposed to stay home in her rural *sítio* and await the team. She didn't, even though Susan had told her three times that she would be there on January 2. The woman's husband was at home, and he explained that no Brazilian would ever have kept the date, so his wife went to town. Well, at least the car worked. The whole team could have been lost. The good news is that they liked the work and got good results in the interviews – no refusals and nine long forms and one short form completed. But, for a first day, it still really couldn't have gone much worse. Susan is tough and took it all well, except she had a good headache.

It wasn't a lot better at home, and Fred lost count of the number of flies he killed. (Fred's father was a genius to send us a fly swatter.) Then at the end of the day, a good-sized spider jumped out not three inches from Fred's hand. The spider is now dead.

With the four o'clock rooster crowing and the cattle being driven out of our highlands back to the plains in the predawn hours, the night is short.

1/04/90: Susan is in Lower Calos right now. The mango fruit is dropping like crazy – all night long, like bombs, from as high as thirty or forty feet. Susan took four bags of twenty each to her interviewers, as there are no mango trees on the *sertão*. On the *sertão*, people have to buy mangos in stores, yet here they are so prolific they rot on the ground. The cashew fruit has disappeared; that season is over.

Remarkably, many people here in Upper Calos haven't even been to Santa Rosa, seventeen miles away, in years.

Evening: All went well for the interview team today, thank goodness. The Lower Calos piece is well on its way, with three good interviewers and one whom Susan is going to let go. That interviewer appears to have a poor attitude about life and is not a

208

team player. She made everybody wait forty-five minutes for her when she could have continued her interview tomorrow. Apparently, many people are interested in the job now that word has gotten around about Susan's presence.

A funny thing that recently happened is that one of the interviewers from the Upper Calos team, who has continued doing interviews of a special group above and beyond the original random sample, had someone say to her, "We heard you were asking about the size of our husbands' penises!" And she was serious. The interviewer loved it, and she and Susan got a good laugh.

1/07/90: Susan is very occupied with collection of data in Lower Calos and analysis of data collected in Upper Calos. She is knee-deep in questionnaires.

1/10/90: Things are going well here. Susan continues commuting to Lower Calos every afternoon, car willing, to drive her team to the remote areas. She takes the back road, which is shorter in distance; it goes directly down the mountain from Upper Calos to Lower Calos, rather than going through Santa Rosa. But the road is much more rudimentary. The ride is forty-five minutes each way over narrow cobblestone mountain roads that are full of potholes. The team is working out very well, including the woman Susan was thinking of letting go. By the end of January, Susan should be finished with the outback and be able to let the team go on their own to do the in-town interviews. She will not have to commute every day. Just in time, too, as the rains will be in full force then, making the roads impassable.

1/11/90: The work in Lower Calos continues to go well. The team is finding a much greater number of tubal ligations, even in the rural areas, so Susan is glad she is doing the comparison of the towns. Incidence of tubal ligations (female sterilization) is an important part of her research on contraception.

1/19/90: Susan continues to go daily to Lower Calos, putting on between eighty and one hundred kilometers each day. Local people are amazed at a woman doing this, particularly alone, so much so that yesterday they sent someone's mother along with Susan when she had to leave the team to go on an errand. The daily trip will probably end next week, since the team is very efficient. They will be done with the rural areas well in advance of the rains. So far, the team has met with only one refusal; the woman in question hid from the interviewers, for whatever reason. In Upper Calos, refusals were at five percent or so, still low for surveys, but in Lower Calos, it has been only one out of one hundred fifty women so far, an excellent rate.

Susan had a tough day early in the week (actually, all of them have been tough because we have had daily flat tires). She was walking into a remote area for an interview and slipped on a fresh "meadow muffin." She fell and got cow dung all over her leg and skirt. She continued after a quick, slightly effective rinse in a stream. And she got the interview! After the interview she "split the herd" as a cattle drive swirled around her on her return. That would have been a marvelous photograph.

We are already planning what will probably be our last trip to Fortaleza before we depart.

Every day, Susan brings home things that she receives as presents, in exchange for delivering mangos by the dozens to the people in Lower Calos. We've received cauliflower leaves, fruit, a strutting guinea hen, sugarcane honey and eggs.

1/26/90: The team finished with the rural interviews in Lower Calos this week. The timing was good, because the rainy season started three days ago, bringing with it a flock of moths (one family of moths even hatched in our car); two gigantic toads that act like doormats in front of the porch; cooler weather; and leaks. But the problems we had last year, when we arrived in mid-February, one month into an exceptionally wet rainy season, are going to be much fewer this year, since most of the leaks in our house have been fixed. We won't be living in a wet house, unlike the one we moved into. Last year, we had mold on almost everything, which was really disturbing. We think we can keep the inside of our already dry house dry throughout the rains, and we can avoid what was really a rough, depressing time.

1/30/90: Fred had some photos developed lately. The one of the car with the entire Upper Calos interview team on board is nice; a good part of the tire disappears up into the wheel well. Too many people to carry is one reason why the field research has been hard on the car. Other good photos are of our neighbor Alfredo planting his bean crop, burning the field and shucking corn. We have lots of nice "people" shots as well. We need to take some photos of the interior of our house before time gets away from us.

Susan is working at home today, since the research assistants in Lower Calos go out interviewing on their own. A college student prepares maps of the blocks in Lower Calos that were selected in the random sample and assigns them to the teams. The work is going well, even better than in Upper Calos, largely because the kidnapping scare that shook the country last August and September has subsided.

2/01/90: The team has now completed about forty percent of the survey in Lower Calos. Susan goes there twice a week for supervision. All of this is a big relief, since she had two threats hanging over her all through January: The arrival of the winter rains would have made the rural roads impassable, and the impending shortage of alcohol for car fuel would have made transportation to rural areas problematic. Neither threat eventuated up until now, thank goodness. She hopes to have all five hundred interviews done by early March.

2/04/90: Susan is almost halfway through with the five-hundred-household fertility survey in Lower Calos. The work is going very well.

2/07/90: Susan is in Lower Calos today. So far only two women have refused interviews, both women who the interviewer had advised wouldn't talk under any circumstances, no matter what the subject. Susan actually believes now that she is going to finish. I guess after so many years the light at the end of the tunnel takes a while to see. Regina has become a good research assistant. She is already finished with a good deal of analysis of the Upper Calos data. Though she only has a fourth-grade education, she is smart, organized and careful. Susan is not relaxed yet, but almost! Without a doubt we still plan to carry all the completed questionnaires (one thousand times fourteen pages) on the plane with us, the only safe way to do it. That will be reams of paper.

3/17/90: Susan is off delivering some of the prizes from the lottery. She was unable to pay the Lower Calos interviewers on Friday, but they apparently expected that a payday was unlikely. Everyone is in the same boat. Susan had to let one of her interviewers go, because she was quite poor at writing up the interviews. As a result, completion of the interviews will take a bit longer than expected, probably three more weeks, until mid-April. But Susan has already begun her other qualitative research interviews, so the delay should not hurt.

3/30/90: Susan delivered two other lottery prizes. It seems that one recipient, a twenty-two-year-old woman who was very poor, had never received a present before. She just stared, no "thank you," no "come in and sit down." She obviously needed the present, but no one had ever shown her how to receive a gift. She wasn't even excited – she was just sort of there. The experience was very moving and sad.

4/16/90: Susan is in Lower Calos today finishing up. We are planning a ten-day car trip through the *sertão* to Salvador da Bahia plus a four-day trip to Recife. Part of this trip will be to visit the haunts of the famous Brazilian bandit and folk hero Lampião.

59: The Continuing Saga of the Car

1/03/90: A fellow came by on Sunday and offered Fred NCz$15,000 for the car, which is a bit more than $500. He said he would give us the money now, and we could give him the car when we are through with it. We don't feel comfortable driving someone else's car. Also, even in the bank, the money would only keep up with inflation and not earn anything. Third, if they solve the alcohol "crisis," the value of the car will go up. Fred promised the man he would talk to him before anyone else when the time comes, but there's still a lot of time to go. It seems, though, that we won't have a problem selling the car after all.

1/30/90: An improvement has been made to the trail we walked to get to the car when it broke down one evening and the team had to leave it overnight. The trail has been made into a road – a fair-weather road, but a road all the same. We drove up to the top of it today. Nice view, but the first good rains and kiss it good-bye!

The rains still haven't come. We had a cloudy sky this morning, but now the sky is clear blue. It's windy, so in spite of the climbing temperature the day is very nice. The cool at night makes up for the heat of the day.

2/13/90: Fred is writing this while sitting at the car shop. He is the first in line. In fact, it's so early that he is the only one in line. But we have to get some work done on the car before we go to Recife. Even if you're second or third in line, you sometimes get thrown into the afternoon. Santa Rosa is actually cool this time of day. All the kids are going to school. They start early to get out before the heat hits.

Two unforgettable images provide redeeming aspects to Fred's bus trip last Sunday. In Santa Rosa it was raining very hard, and a boy was walking along from drainpipe to drainpipe. Drainpipes here come off structures at roof level and usually extend from one to four feet out. The boy was showering for about five seconds under each drainpipe; he even began to dance under one! The second image was of one girl cradling her bus-sick friend's head in her arms. Both images were very endearing. The bus trip was worth those images.

Here comes the body shop owner to open up.

The computers are down at the bank, at least until ten a.m., they say. So, Fred can't make any purchases. He is glad he took a book with him.

3/06/90: Susan is getting ready to go to Lower Calos for the morning. The car is all set, having had a new exhaust system installed (again) yesterday. The whole thing fell off on Friday at about five thirty p.m., as Susan was returning from Lower Calos. Luckily, the bus driver for the Lower Calos route happened by in a pick-up truck and hauled the pieces to his house. Fred picked them up on Saturday. He was able to get the pieces into the car trunk after bending them at a series of three or four gashes in one of the pipes. Some of the system was salvageable, but the major parts were not. The car roared like a tank all weekend, but it's purring now.

Well, we were wrong about the car purring. It just had a flat.

60: Graduation Time

1/06/90: Fred attended the *aula de saudade* (class session of remembrance, longing, old times) of the eighth-grade class that graduates this year. (Graduations are in December or January in this part of Brazil.) Vanda, the interviewer from Upper Calos who has the most education, is in the class. She teaches third grade and is just graduating from eighth grade. She has six children and is thirty-five years old. She attends class in the morning and teaches class in the afternoon. More power to her. No one attaches any stigma to the presence of older people in lower-level classes. The night classes are loaded with older students, many in their early to late twenties. Because of the age difference, on school game days the night students typically roundly defeat the day students. The day students put up with it, but they don't like it.

The *aula de saudade* started about an hour after it was supposed to. It featured loud music and various presentations of talent by students, including mouthing popular songs and doing coordinated movements. In a "secret friend" gift exchange, every student got up to give a gift to another whose name was drawn from a hat. The giver had to describe the person, to see if the recipient could guess, but even after the class members had spent several years together, givers gave mostly physical descriptions. Only Vanda described the traits of her secret friend. Could this be because of a notion of privacy – we have seen little evidence of that here – an inability to discern traits, a conscious distancing or something else? So often the color of the student's skin came up, with people describing their classmates as "very dark" or "light," for example. This part of the ceremony took forever.

Then the students asked for someone from the faculty to say something. Nobody moved, and the students wanted Fred to speak. Everyone says he spoke well, but people are so polite. Fred has no idea of the quality of his words, but his quantity was short!

The students danced afterward, and Fred tried his best at the local step, the *forró*. When he headed home, he had five people in the back seat. Fred was in the front seat with a load of luggage. Fred doesn't ask questions anymore. He just drives the bus. Guess what he has to show for it today? A flat tire!

1/08/90: Last night was the second half of the graduation of the eighth grade, the formal part. It started with a mass, which began forty-five minutes late. Vanda was very glad that Susan attended. Fred again got a special honor and sat up front with the dignitaries to hand out diplomas. The whole event lasted over three hours.

Classes may not begin until March because of *Carnaval*, but they may go straight through July. Students don't need more vacation time than they already get. The preparations for *Carnaval* again remind us that we've come full circle, since last year we arrived in Brazil just a few weeks before *Carnaval*.

61: Money Troubles, Part Three

1/05/90: Inflation has been out of this world. It topped one thousand seven hundred percent for 1989. Over three months, the exchange rate went from NCz$4.50 to NCz$30.00 to the dollar. One of the economic experts said that the economy is <u>not</u> out of control, because people know what to expect each month, plus there are built-in monthly adjustments that everyone is used to making. But, even at the jobs where the owners are good at applying the adjustments, prices have already risen for a whole month before the adjustments are made. The result is that every month, a few owners are making an additional "inflation profit" over and above regular profit margins. Some owners are glibly saying in interviews that they like inflation. But perhaps the market is responding. The price of meat shot up so much that some meat stores now have no customers.

1/26/90: Prices have skyrocketed here. But so has the dollar, thank goodness. We got NCz$35.50 to the dollar today, for Susan to pay her interviewers' salaries in Lower Calos.

2/09/90: The dollar hit NCz$48.50 last Wednesday! The "overnight" accounts in the bank, where you can deposit money for just a night, are earning 100.2 percent at the monthly rate. That's over three percent a night! The dollar has already gone up over thirty-five percent this month. You can double your money in a month but not be able to buy anything more with it because prices will have also doubled. The problem for the poor is that wages are a month behind, so wage earners can buy this month what people with money in the overnight accounts bought last month. Too much!

3/09/90: Everyone is raising their prices now, expecting a price freeze when Collor de Melo takes office next Friday.

3/17/90: The government closed all the banks on Wednesday. They will remain closed through the weekend, as people were withdrawing their money in record amounts as a "safeguard" against any new government policy. And yesterday was the day! The new economic plan of Collor was unveiled with plenty of twists and turns, the consequences of which even the economists have no idea, but everyone seems to hope that it will work.

There is now another new currency, the *Cruzeiro* (abbreviated Crz). It is our third currency since we arrived in Brazil. In addition, there are freezes on prices and salaries, as well as a freeze on funds in the bank, limiting how much money one can withdraw. The currency has been devalued by ten percent, and the official dollar market is now free floating, rather than dictated by the Bank of Brasil. Also, the country is now open to all foreign goods, in contrast to the monopolies that have been in place, which made for large profits for many industries. And Collor had promised in no uncertain terms that there would be no freeze! Also surprising for us, none of these measures needs to be approved by the legislature.

But the owners anticipated a freeze nevertheless. Right before the change of currency, the price of alcohol for the car went from NCz$18 to NCz$28 per liter overnight. All prices have been ordered rolled back to Monday's prices. People have already been arrested for changing prices. The inflation rate for March, just the first half, was eighty percent! The attempts to

219

gouge and squeeze are the major problems here. Some good, honest competition will be good for everyone.

The week promises to be interesting, as people start to figure out what it all means. The plan is all-encompassing and will affect everybody in some way, but it seems to be geared toward the rich, forcing them to use their money for development and production.

3/21/90: Brazil has gone overnight from one of the cheapest countries to live in to one of the most expensive. The day Collor was inaugurated, he put in a sweeping comprehensive economic package that strikes hardest at the ten percent of the population considered elites. Many of the rich had just been putting their money into overnight accounts or bought dollars, just playing with their money rather than using it for production or factory improvements to increase productivity – or wages, for that matter. The overnight accounts were earning as much as three percent per day.

People were withdrawing money in great quantities beginning Monday of inauguration week, in such amounts that a meeting Tuesday night of heads of banks convinced Collor to ask President Sarney to close the banks as of Wednesday. Sarney complied, and the banks closed from inauguration day on Wednesday through the weekend. To top it off, the banks in Ceará were also closed on Monday for a Saint's Day.

One measure allowed withdrawal of a maximum of NCz$50,000 (about $625 at the time) from overnight accounts, with remaining money frozen for eighteen months! Another froze prices of necessities, lowered some, but let luxury items hit new highs. Alcohol for cars went from eighteen to twenty-eight *Cruzeiros*. The *Cruzado Novo* has been done away with. Then, as a result of the freezing of the overnight accounts, liquidity disappeared, and the dollar on the parallel market dropped from eighty-two to anywhere from thirty-five to forty-five. The rate has been fluctuating so much that no one really knows what one will actually get for a dollar. The combination of item prices going up plus the dollar plummeting has really been a double whammy. A tank of gas cost U.S. $25 today; previously that had cost U.S. $8.50. The salaries of Susan's interview team in Lower Calos went up about forty percent. The salaries will not go up past that level, since salaries do not go up until April 1, by which time the team will be finished.

The plan may just do what this country needs, at least a first step and a big one. The banks have a great deal of money to loan now. Collor has personally stepped in to stop a company from dismissing a large group of workers. The prices that have been allowed a jump are on items that are not available or needed by the poorer segment: fuel for cars, records and tapes, beer and whisky. All restrictions on imports were lifted, providing the much-needed competition that businesses need. Several state-run industries will be privatized, Petrobras, the fuel company, being one of the biggest.

We went to Santa Rosa yesterday to see if anyone wanted dollars, but no one had any money. Everyone is in the same boat. When we got home, the power was out. We were ready to pack!

As of Monday, we had NCz$6 to our name in Brazilian currency – about ten cents! Plus, we owed money all over Santa Rosa. This is not a problem, since most people run up a tab and pay at the end of the month. During inflationary times, the store clerks write down the items someone buys and apply the current price when they pay up. With the freeze, not paying was less of a problem, but we don't like to owe.

When in conversation with our neighbor Sônia, one of Susan's interviewers, she heard that we only had NCz$6, she thought we meant that we only had NCz$6,000, since people often use shorthand for thousands. When Susan clarified, Sônia was shocked and offered to lend us NCz$500 so we could at least buy fuel for our car.

At worst, we were going to ask a friend for money. We thought maybe the bank in Santa Rosa would change money at the official rate. We stopped there before we called our friend. We were told what we expected to hear, that the bank in Santa Rosa does not change money, that we would need to go to the Bank of Brasil in Fortaleza, but... but... there were people who work in the bank who were willing to buy dollars at the parallel rate! The bank guard took us over to the women who apparently are always buying dollars. Susan said that, knowing Brazil, she shouldn't be surprised, but even she was shocked.

We walked right around the lines (bank lines have been going around blocks since yesterday) to the desks of the women. They were all set! We thought we should at least sit down and be less conspicuous, but no one seemed to care that this irregular transaction was going on. We sold $500 at fifty per dollar. The women wrote checks, went behind the tellers, cashed the checks, gave us the money and away we went, leaving two other employees with long faces who got in on it too late. "Is that all you have to sell?" they lamented.

Everyone hopes Collor's plan will work, because the country needs a real shake-up to get it on the right track. Everyone knows this. The ten percent of the population that this affects the most, the rich, aren't that big a voting bloc. As one local merchant put it, everyone has to make sacrifices to help the country change.

3/30/90: The value of used cars has plummeted. A 1983 Chevette, about the same car as our 1983 Voyage, was offered for Crz$70,000 and did not sell even at that low price. Before the economic plan, that sort of car would sell for at least Crz$200,000. So, the drop in value has been about two-thirds! Maybe by the end of April the market will rebound.

4/04/90: Fortaleza was hot! And expensive! Tourism will die completely if something doesn't change. The hotel where we usually stay was asking $100 a night. We bargained with the clerk at the desk until we got a fifty percent discount, which, at $50 a night, was still $15 to $20 more than we paid previously at the same hotel. Plus, the hotel was almost empty. At the restaurant on the beach that we always go to, our meal cost $18. We usually pay about $12. And for $18 all we got was a pizza, when we usually get two full-plate dinners of fish and beef for $12. There are better places for tourists to go with their dollars. If Brazil isn't cheap, no one is going to come.

4/07/90: The official dollar is now a floating dollar, so there is no official parallel market at present.

4/18/90: The new president's economic plan has affected us financially. The dollar should be at one hundred fifteen to the *Cruzeiro* to be about where we were before the plan, but the dollar has stalled at around fifty-five to sixty. Everything is costing us double. But, considering that our rent, which in our time here has never been raised by the owner, went from $2.50 to $5.00, we can't really complain. The plan has put an end to all the speculation that was going on, particularly around the dollar, which was being played like a stock market. Tourism has already slowed drastically, as Brazil has priced itself out of being a bargain for tourists. The prices for food and most goods are frozen. But because no one has any money, since even salaries can't be met in some instances – where funds for salaries are frozen – the shelves are stocked for the first time in a long time. Ironically, the shelves are full, but the stores are empty.

4/19/90: One more economic note. The newspaper has an article about how people are dealing with having their money frozen. Apparently, any extra money that people now have, instead of going to the purchase of dollars, is going to the purchase of the frozen funds, which people are selling the rights to, since they can't get the money out for eighteen months. The frozen money is the old money, the *Cruzado Novo*. The currency now is the *Cruzeiro*. At any rate, it appears that people are selling the frozen money for half its value in order to gain some liquidity in *Cruzeiros*. It is a gamble, since the frozen money could disappear. It is speculators feeding on speculators.

62: All Play and No Work

1/20/90: Incredibly, because *Carnaval* isn't until late February this year, the authorities have postponed the opening of school here from the beginning of February until March 5. Students will then not take the usual July break. The students don't like that, and parents have complained that too much school in a stretch of time is bad. No one here seems serious about much. The energy around samba schools continues. We are party poopers, as we see a lot of energy, money and national concentration going into an activity that is not the most worthwhile, in our view.

Alfredo's brother is having a party at his *bodega* tonight, only about two hundred yards down the way, so the music and noise carry to our house. A major landowner here is only paying his workers the equivalent of U.S. $0.50 a day, so the men will not have much money to buy drinks, and the party should not go on too long. That's less than one-fourth of the minimum salary required by law. A wife of one of those workers visited us today, bringing a dozen avocados. It was painful to see how very needy she is.

An advertisement for the post office caught our attention. It shows a little yellow steamer chugging up one of the byways of the Amazon to deliver mail. This country really could be something. Fred is reading a history of Brazil now, and all the quotes keep referring to Brazil's great "potential," quotes beginning as early as 1520 and still running up to today. Brazil is still all potential, with so few realizing their potential while the few take it all for themselves.

2/27/90: The rains came in torrents last night, pretty well wiping out any celebrations. We had planned to drop in at Berí's bar, since he was having a *trio eléctrico* play, for which he had paid NCz$9,000 (almost U.S. $160), a sum he can ill afford. They tried to get something started. We could hear them until the electricity went out at about ten p.m. The band packed up and went home. Everyone had planned to go, and all were waiting for the rains to stop, but it ended up that just the usual people showed up – the fellows that always hang out there with just enough money to buy a couple of fingers of *pinga*. Rain never stops them. In fact, the rain didn't stop until early this morning. The last time Berí tried to hold such an event, the electricity went out also. The bar has a covered porch, but the porch is smaller than most kitchens in the U.S. It is a sad hard-luck story.

63: A Champion Retires

1/27/90: Fred played volleyball today, after running about two kilometers yesterday. It was too much, and he is stiff. Susan went running today. She spends so much time in the car that she gets very little exercise. Fred says it feels good to be stiff, but it didn't take too much to make him feel this way.

2/04/90: Healthwise, it has been a good year for Fred. He probably has added ten years to his life by coming here. He is well rested and has lost weight, even after drinking his share of beer. He is now at one hundred seventy-two pounds, having come here at two hundred twenty. And his blood pressure is well into the normal range.

2/07/90: Fred went to volleyball this morning. The balls were flat, and no one had a needle. Fred had bought two a while back, but one got lost two days after he bought it, and the other one broke yesterday. How does one break a needle? He drove all over town (that doesn't take too long), stopping and asking if anyone had a needle. No luck. He is going to buy three this time and sleep with two of them. The ones he bought in the States don't fit the pump.

Fred's team travels about eighty kilometers this Sunday to a town in the *sertão* to play. Fred is driving, but the team is going on town trucks. Three teams are going: volleyball, handball and salon football. Volleyball should be the first sport played, since the sun's position affects the game. They hope to be back by noon.

2/10/90: No volleyball practice today, just swimming – if you like shallow pools! Tomorrow, the team heads to a town halfway to Fortaleza for a volleyball/salon football/handball meet. Rather than subject the car to the trip, Fred changed his mind and decided to go on the team "bus." They leave at five thirty a.m., since they need to finish all the games before it gets too hot. If it rains, it will only rain for a short time, and the heat will dry it all up in no time after any shower. Volleyball will be played first, before the sun gets too high in the sky.

2/12/90: Well, a three-hour bus trip ended with two games of volleyball that lasted a total of about one-half hour. The team lost, 15–3 and 15–4. Fred could tell when they warmed up that no one was with it. A lot of factors are involved, but a big part of it is a lack of practice in concentrating. Life here in Upper Calos doesn't really call for it, and it's evident that concentration is not required in schools. The volleyball team wasn't alone in its loss. The handball team lost 13–1, the salon football team 3–1.

The other volleyball team was better no doubt. Fred doesn't mind losing so much if they have had a chance to play their best. This was simple self-destruction. In the first game, the team had nine first serves hit the net or go flying out of bounds. They didn't even get to play! Fred is still upset, but the lads were all fine by the time of the handball game. They are good kids, but the experience was frustrating.

The bus picked Fred up at six thirty a.m., though it was supposed to come by at five thirty. He was back by three p.m. He showered, and we went to Berí and Sônia's new home restaurant for breakfast-lunch-dinner. The food was very good. We will make this a regular practice. It was a nice break.

Though it rained all day yesterday, today is a beautiful day, like a Canadian summer afternoon. The air is clear with a hint of coolness. It's probably about sixty-six degrees. Susan just returned from running, so Fred is going now. He already changed the flat tire on the car.

2/25/90: Berí, Sônia's husband, is playing in his last soccer game today, so we will go. How they will play on the wet field remains to be seen. Soccer in the mud isn't quite the same game.

We are back from the soccer game. The field is on a slope, so it was as dry as a bone and as hard as a rock. All six goals in the game were scored uphill. The game was decided on penalty kicks. Berí's team lost 5–4 on the kicks. The fans were brutal, laughing at the misplays. It is clear that not all Brazilians are naturals at soccer. It was a team of *velhos* (oldsters), but it was still fun to watch. A nice ceremony took place after the game. They gave Berí a trophy, and he handed a new pair of shoes over to the person who is replacing him on the team – although no one on either team wore shoes during the game, which made our feet hurt just to watch. Berí made a speech, extolling his own virtues as a player. They had a band and tons of people in attendance, mostly to see the two games that came after, but most people were attentive during the ceremony. Sônia could not be happier that he's quitting. There are lots of broken legs every season.

We had a hard time understanding anything anybody said. All the men, even the players, were feeling no pain, and the noise of the band was an interference. The car was full coming home, since six young people asked us for a ride.

3/09/90: We are scheduled to play volleyball in three weeks. These days the court is always wet and slippery.

64: Take a Chance and Get a Goat

1/28/90: Today is a slow Sunday with showers. We went to Upper Calos town for the goat lottery. Our agronomist friend had acquired fifty goats, and people had to register for the lottery. Some little goats had just been born, so that was a bonus for winners, who would get both the mother goat and the kid. The lottery was fun, except we got "hit up" for money from about six people, which we refused to give or we would be sucked dry. It was probably because more poor people were in town for the lottery. We know the need, but this method gets upsetting.

2/25/90: We visited our agronomist friend and his wife this morning at their *sítio*. He has a beautiful garden with a little bit of everything growing like crazy. He has a disagreement with the mayor. The mayor supported the goat distribution idea but decided not to follow through with a program to help the winners learn to take care of their goats. Many of the winners live in Upper Calos town and, as town folk, don't know how to take care of animals.

After all this today, we closed our gate early. Any visits or any more socializing today would be too much.

65: Trying to Make a Go of It

2/04/90: We went to the new *bodega* of our neighbors, Berí and Sônia. Sônia was one of the interviewers for Upper Calos and is a very good cook. Berí tore down his old *bodega* as soon as he had his new house-cum-*bodega* open for business. He has tables and a patio. It was fun. We only spent U.S. $3.60 eating out in January, so we deserved a meal out as February begins. The meal, which was a very typical one for Ceará, cost a total of U.S. $5.91. We may have our going-away party there.

2/25/90: We went to Sônia and Berí's for lunch again today. Sônia really does put out a nice spread, with beans and rice, of course, plus an excellent chicken dish, noodles in a butter sauce, mashed potatoes and *farofa*, all for about $4.50. We bought them a blackboard, chalk and eraser as a bar-warming present, and it is hanging out with all the prices. You have to do prices in chalk here. The place was packed with all the men of the neighborhood, all drunk. Unfortunately, that is a common occurrence on Sundays, the only morning men do not work. One man was asleep, with his head on a table. Another, who fell at least twice on the way according to reports we received, sat down next to Susan and started to talk to her, but it is impossible to understand what people are saying when they are lit. Once the food is served, people leave you alone. It's nice to have a decent restaurant so close.

3/11/90: Fred got back in time to go to our regular Sunday lunch at Sônia and Berí's place. Sônia loves for us to come, as

231

we are her only customers who, as far as we can see, order a whole meal and not just rice and beans (and there are very few of those smaller meals served, too). Sônia tries out different sauces with us, mostly with chicken but sometimes with turkey. The locals can't support a restaurant at all, and the "tourists," that is, the absentee landlords, are not used to having a restaurant here, so they don't stop. It is sort of interesting to eat lunch with three dogs at your feet. If Sônia and Berí stick with it, they should do all right.

3/30/90: Last Sunday, because we were at Sônia and Beri's restaurant and their landowner and his family were there as well, a doctor and his family saw the "crowd" and also stopped to eat. Sônia only has enough plates for one table at a time, so she kept sending the kids to peek to see if we were done eating. Then yesterday, Sônia asked Susan if Susan thought she provided good portions and enough variety of food and if she served it well. Sônia was all nervous and hoping she had done a good job for the doctor's family. Apparently, they were her first "real" customers. The whole episode was very sweet. We had purchased some plates, six for about $3, for the Lower Calos lottery, but after this exchange with Sônia, we decided Sônia could better use them. Sônia was thrilled. These little things keep the fun going for us here.

4/15/90: Happy Easter! We had a fairly quiet Sunday, except for the fellows returning from midnight mass at two fifteen a.m., who laid on the horn to wake up our neighbor so they could get some more to drink. Alfredo obliged and opened up his *bodega*. Fred was ready to go after them with the bat! We went to Sônia's again for lunch. All the tables were taken after we got the last one. Sônia was very happy, except she ran out of gas for the stove. That delayed everything for about half an hour. No problem.

66: Back to School

2/04/90: With school not starting until March 5, Fred has had lots of free time and is reading some books he brought along that he has wanted to read for years. Since he is feeling well, he is running on that nice, soft dirt road. He walks down to the road, runs about two kilometers on the road, then runs/walks home. Volleyball on Saturdays and Wednesdays and the running combine to make a good exercise regime for him. Susan runs occasionally but is really tied to those questionnaires – reviewing, evaluating, clarifying. When she finally has her doctorate, she will have a new life, with no more classes or papers.

3/11/90: The first day of school was a week ago Friday and was a typical Brazilian show. Fred had to inquire the day before when the English classes were scheduled, since no one had informed him. There were no planning days like in the U.S., and the next day, the first day, Professor Z. did not show up. Fred felt obligated to go and show the students what they have a right to expect. Well, Professor Z. wasn't the only teacher missing. Fifteen minutes into Fred's second hour, the administrator went to him and asked if he would stop his current class and switch to another that he was to teach last period, since the teacher for the intervening class had not shown up. If Fred did that, according to this proposal, then those students in the other class could go home early while Fred returned to the class that he had already started and would have had to wait for his return. Fred didn't switch.

Classes were missing anywhere from eight to thirty-six books, students not having returned the books from the previous year. The electricity went out, though not for long. The community center, about thirty feet away, was blaring rock music from about third period on. Then, before the last class, the administrator asked if Fred could let the class go early, after twenty minutes or so, since everybody was tired. From what? Oh, my.

3/15/90: Regina, one of Susan's research assistants, will probably just return to her old teaching job when we leave. She teaches at the local school down in our *sítio*, which goes up to fourth grade and is run by nuns based in Santa Rosa. The pay is NCz$100 per month, or about U.S. $1.20 per month. That is 1/36 of the legal minimum salary. Even here that buys nothing.

That the school run by the nuns only goes up to the fourth grade is the major reason why most people around our area only have a fourth-grade education. Many parents are reluctant to send their children into Upper Calos town for the upper grades.

Fred tried to make it to English class last night. Last Friday, we had a power outage after everyone had arrived at school, so they had only forty-five minutes of class after more than an hour of travel for many of the students. Then last night, the power went out for twenty minutes before Fred was set to leave home. He went into town to check on things, passed the two trucks that carry students between the outer areas and town, stopped at the school to see if the director was going to complain to the power company (he wasn't) and found out his Friday class had been moved to Thursday! We are sure the power is diverted to someplace else, a factory in Santa Rosa or similar. The

234

complacency is getting us down. We are betting the power goes out tonight, too.

3/26/90: Fred went to Professor Z.'s school in Santa Rosa to visit some of the classes and speak to the students. He got home about eleven p.m. The school is much nicer than the school in Upper Calos. Students pay the equivalent of U.S. $22 per month in tuition. Fred saw three students from Upper Calos that he had in class last year who are now taking classes there. They commute every night back and forth from Upper Calos to Santa Rosa. Fred is not so sure the education is that much better at the Santa Rosa school. Class size was still too large, one class with sixty students.

Fred felt like an animal in a zoo, a curiosity. He talked about his impressions of Brazil and answered questions. Many students wanted his response to Collor's plan for the economy. Others wanted him to compare the level of Brazilian education to that of the U.S. They asked for the truth, so Fred told it to them. He thinks they already knew. Fred enjoyed the opportunity, but five classes in a row of forty minutes each taxed his Portuguese. No one tried to speak any English, even though these were English classes. The students never get a chance to practice spoken English, it seems, and the emphasis is on reading English. That is a mistake.

Last Friday at school, a nice thing happened. One class, one of the small ones that Fred had last year also, was writing exercises on the board. They were reading the phrases, and their pronunciation was very good. Fred got satisfaction from that. Only having one day of classes and one class at night is much better. Last year he tried to do too much and didn't enjoy it as much.

3/30/90: Susan is in Lower Calos for what should be her last review of interviews. On Wednesday night, we went to Lower Calos to a class that one of Susan's interviewers teaches. The students had some good questions and wanted our impressions of Brazil. We enjoyed it. We were told the class would run from eight until eight forty-five, but it started at eight twenty and went until nine forty-five! (Today in Upper Calos, they changed the schedule again on Fred and no one told him. It really is amazing.)

4/18/90: Fred taught English class tonight. No one studies. There is no tradition of studying, particularly among students in the night classes. The teachers don't push it, which cheapens the efforts of the students who have the wits and energy to try to learn something. The teachers don't even settle at the middle but teach to the bottom. Cheating (interestingly, called *pescando*, or fishing) is so blatant and tolerated it drives Fred nuts. When he mentions this to other teachers, they just shrug their shoulders. The prevailing sense is that no one believes they are going anywhere, so whether they cheat or not makes no difference. It is frustrating and sad.

Students don't have confidence they have potential, let alone have any frustrations at not being able to reach it. Fred has come across so many good, bright kids, as bright as he has seen in the U.S. gifted programs where he has worked. But the bright kids here don't even know they are bright and don't have any idea what is available to do with their intelligence – because there isn't anything to motivate them here. There are about forty students he would like to take to the U.S., but they are going nowhere. This is very sad.

67: A Rare Theft

2/04/90: There was a real shock in Upper Calos town over the weekend. Someone stole the electric motor from a water pump. Everyone was talking about it. The modern world, unfortunately, seems to have arrived. We will be interested to see if they find the culprit or if the motor just "returns." Our guess is that the culprit is a local, who probably sold it in Santa Rosa. If it were put into use around here, everyone would know right away. But sometimes burglars are not very bright.

68: Rain and Crops

2/04/90: Everyone here wishes the rains would begin. The first planting of beans is on the verge of being completely lost. Last year, too much rain destroyed the crop… this year, too little has delayed it. Some water-resource planning would be valuable here. There is enough water, but it just is not managed at all.

2/07/90: We have a bunch of bananas that are just perfectly ripened right now and delicious, but there are about sixty of them. We have them coming out of our ears.

2/09/90: It's raining now, pretty steadily if not hard. It's very nice. We think the rainy season has begun. Some thunder just clapped, and the rain is coming harder. Susan is in Lower Calos, but very likely it isn't raining there, and the route back is all paved with cobblestones.

2/10/90: The rainy season has definitely started. It is raining steadily now, raining or threatening to rain all day long. But we are way ahead of when we moved in. All the leaks that had deluged the house a month before we moved in are stopped, so we start out dry. We feel the difference.

2/25/90: The weather since Friday (it is now Sunday) has had a fair dose of rain every day. We've moved the clothesline in under the porch, but things from yesterday still aren't dry today. That was a problem last year, always two days behind in the drying, particularly with the diapers. Everything is all *Carnaval*. The streets are loaded, as are the people in the streets! It will be a relief when *Carnaval* is over. Everything is closed except the bars.

3/09/90: Once Berí built his new *bodega*, he tore down his old one in short order. The tile on the new one is covered with stucco and looks much better than the old one, although it appears that all these constructions weather poorly, with chips and water stains. Still, the new bar is certainly a step up. The rains have let up for three days now; the beans and corn still look good. Those who planted too early suffered and had to replant. Every year here is iffy for crops. Everyone thinks the rains are here to stay.

3/30/90: It's harvest time for beans. We got a present of some fresh ones that have not been laid in the sun to dry, and they are still green. You need to cook them pretty quickly after picking or they sprout, but they are easy to make, since they don't need soaking. They cook up in about an hour and a half and are quite delicious and tender. Susan, not much of a bean eater, even had seconds. The rains have been a bit weak but enough to bring in a decent crop, better than last year's destroyed crop, for sure. These fresh beans are only available during a few weeks of the year. We made the mistake of telling the person who gave us the fresh beans how delicious they were, and a twenty-pound bag of them showed up the next day on our porch. We ate what we could and gave the rest away.

69: Animal Welfare

1/06/90: This was a beautiful evening – the type of evening that if you could find a place that had days like this you would move there forever in a heartbeat. All was quiet on the road below, except at five thirty p.m., our neighbor Alfredo had to drive his cows through their usual grazing areas, because the one new mother cow had hidden her calf in the undergrowth somewhere as protection. A half hour later, all arrived safe and sound, mother and calf reunited. The newborn is a beautiful brown male calf with big brown eyes. Alfredo sold a cow yesterday, to be slaughtered for meat at our usual place. He got the equivalent of U.S. $73 for it.

2/04/90: A mother hen and nine chicks are trooping across the front porch. They are cute – five black chicks and four yellow, but they leave presents! Fred moved them on.

2/09/90: Our handyman Raimundo always stays here when we travel, so he handles any invasions by ants, and ant invasions are too commonplace to even tell about. The ceiling always shows wet spots after a heavy rain, as do the walls. The stucco acts more like a sponge, letting water in and out. Raimundo says the stucco won't cave in, never does. Still a mystery! The space between the ceiling and the roof was cleaned out in the spring, and the rats subsequently moved out. It's pretty quiet up there now. Fred had a look around up there, and the space still has lots of lizards and leftover tiles and boards, but it is fairly clean.

The brown calf is doing very well. In addition, the brown cow gave birth to a beautiful brown-and-white calf. All are down in the *sertão* now, since the rain and flies seem to come at the same time and drive the cows nuts.

Three cowboys, real *sertão* cowboys, were up here in the hills leading a bull to one of the *sítios*, perhaps for breeding. Fred got some good pictures of them. That is a rare sight up here. Also, they butchered a sheep in Alfredo's yard during lunchtime, so Fred got some photos of that, too. It's quiet, but not that quiet.

3/11/90: Fred walked into the room we use for storage the other night during yet another power outage and spotted two huge eyes looking at him from inside the broom. It wasn't our live-in frog, who usually is found wedged into a corner. He got closer and saw it was what we would call a mouse, perhaps, but it looked like a miniature opossum, only it had dark fur and was cuter. It was about the size of the head of a soup spoon. Fred grabbed a jar to catch it, scooped along the wall behind the pile of dirty clothes and uncovered another one. He took off the top layer of clothes and found two more, nestled into a shirt and asleep. Still another one turned up in the corner. He caught all five and put them in a box for the night with some rice crispies and closed the cover.

The next day, Regina found one more, which escaped, and still another in the can that holds the clothes pins. They were really cute but had teeth like little saws. We fed them some milk from an eyedropper and, after some initial attacks and bites on the dropper, several of them figured this was food and learned fast to just swallow. Well, this couldn't last, particularly when we found out that their favorite food is clothes. After a day and a half, Fred made a little house for them inside a box. He put in a sponge full of milk and some old socks and newspaper. He cut out a little door on the box, put the whole thing inside a plastic bag and walked it out into the *mata*. He hasn't gone back to check on them, and it has been a week now. He doesn't think he will.

It seems they had lived among the tiles of our roof. That is perhaps one of the reasons snakes like to go up there, to eat the mice, although we have only had the one snake. The critters probably got blown and washed in and down during one of the rain or windstorms we have had. The mother mouse is somewhere, but we have not seen her. It is sad to see them go to their fate, but they bite, and no one wanted them.

Susan had six beautiful mangos on the back porch drying in the sun after being washed. Sometime in the afternoon they disappeared. Mangos are not a food that people need to steal here, plentiful as they are. It was a mystery, until three days later we saw Alfredo's pig out on our parking area inhaling fallen mangos. Mystery solved. The pig, about one hundred twenty-five pounds, is now bacon in Santa Rosa. We bet he tasted great, with just a hint of fruit.

Fred watched them come to take the pig away. What a chore. Did he squeal! They had to toss him up onto the back of a truck, a lift of about 4.5 feet, and he did not like it. He was huge. But Alfredo got about U.S. equivalent $50 for him, one month's minimum salary, and he has little to do to get the pigs to grow. He just lets them wander and eat the natural droppings in the area. A new pig costs about $1, so they give a good return. Also, the price of meat stays right with inflation, even ahead of it sometimes. Ham from pigs in rural areas is much preferred to ham from pigs that root through garbage dumps in towns, so this is a good enterprise for Alfredo.

Susan ran over a two-foot-long poisonous snake with the car last week, killing it. A huge frog got into the bathroom. Rains continue sporadically. Along the road the other evening, we passed by a headless black goat. (Black goats are big in black magic here.) The mangos still drop like bombs all night long. Because of winds in the evening and night, the dogs in the neighborhood get spooked by the sound and bark and howl, disturbing everyone's sleep.

3/26/90: Fred has a bug bite/allergic reaction syndrome again. He has "archipelagos" of bites in several places, probably from gnats, as mosquito bites usually disappear on him in about thirty minutes. He has had the gnat bites for over a week. Something from them must get into his system. His eyelids and earlobes itch like crazy, even though they have no bites on them. And his skin crawls. A woman who works at the health post had all kinds of allergic reactions. She went to Brasilia, the capital, for treatment, and it all cleared up right away. She returned home, and it started all over again. Antihistamines, particularly the one we have, purchased here and probably potent, knock Fred out, but they give relief. Fred has no idea where he got the bites. He hasn't had any new ones, and Susan and Romey weren't bit. You can't even see the little buggers! This is one thing about Brazil we won't miss.

5/11/90: Put this in the same category: Regina was leaving for home yesterday at lunchtime and spotted a two-foot-long snake right in front of the porch. She called Fred, and he smashed it with a bamboo pole. Our neighbor identified the snake as poisonous; she had killed the same type of snake just the other day right behind her house. We have seen about twelve snakes in all our time here and have killed three of them, each of which has been poisonous. Though we are getting almost nonchalant about the sightings, our vigilance continues. Nothing surprises us anymore.

70: Thoughts about Leaving

2/04/90: We are figuring on being back in the States by the end of May, two months later than our original projections for the stay here. There is just too much work to be able to get it all done by March 31.

2/26/90: We have a beautiful day – blue skies and fluffy white clouds. Both of us went running this morning.

We will have a pretty firm idea of our return date by the end of March. It looks more and more like the last week in May. Before we leave, we will spend a week in Fortaleza to sell the car.

Fred's father has been our only guest. Even people from Santa Rosa that we know don't come up here. We invited two people from Fortaleza, who were going on to Tianguá, to stop and visit, but perhaps we were too explicit about our hardships with the bugs and critters and state of the roads, because they never stopped. We are indeed rural.

3/11/90: We may give a thank-you party after Lent. Susan has already come up with a list of over two hundred names of invitees. We will see.

4/03/90: We have our plane reservations for our return home. We will arrive home on May 27.

5/08/90: Since we are going home soon, we have started to pack things up. We are on R and R for a while, saving money by staying here at home, lying low while still tying up loose ends. But there aren't many.

We have had to cancel the trip to Salvador de Bahia because of the weather. We are, however, still squeezing in the four-day trip to Recife. Fred had been very much looking forward to visiting the haunts in the state of Bahia of the bandit Lampião and his apparently ruthless partner Maria Bonita, but it is not meant to be.

71: Stage II Qualitative Research – The Symbols of Life

2/05/90: Right now, Susan is in the midst of preparing the last major piece of research, a type of qualitative probing she will do here in Upper Calos. It focuses on pictures of life here, women's bodies, families and other everyday things. The purpose is to get a grasp of what anthropologists call people's "symbolic universe." You show the pictures and ask the informants to react. Sometimes you ask structured questions. This type of research is much more creative than the type of sociological questions that form the basis of the quantitative work. The hard part is to find the right pictures. Susan gave up on the idea of using photos that Fred might take, because here everyone knows everyone else, and they would therefore be reluctant to say what they really thought about someone's house or family. She is getting photos from books and magazines. This exercise should take most of March.

3/15/90: Susan had the clan over – the interviewers who are doing supplementary interviews with women who had tubal ligations but who weren't in the random sample here in Upper Calos. The clan is Vanda, Naisa and Sônia. The results can't be used statistically with the larger sample, but the information can be used for qualitative analysis. The group conducted a lottery for prizes for the special interview group. The work has revealed a lot of misconceptions about contraceptives. Some women think birth control pills are spermicides and so only take them after intercourse. Then, when they got pregnant, they lost confidence in the pills. Some women thought that a tubal ligation involved tying off the vagina. Health education here has to start with square one. Susan is providing some instruction on the rhythm method for some women, but the task is huge.

Susan has computed from her sample the average number of houses in each *sítio* and the average number of people in each house. This gives an estimated population of about fourteen thousand for the municipality of Upper Calos.

One of the neighbors was in labor, so Susan drove her to the maternity center in Upper Calos town. A tire went flat when Susan got home. At least these things happen when we are driving slowly on the bad roads, although the roads are the reason they happen. She is now in Upper Calos town again, having driven Vanda back home and taken the local cheering club to visit the woman in the maternity center. Chances are that the baby has already been born, and the mother is probably waiting to be driven back home.

Susan is back home. The baby boy had indeed been born before she got there. She suggested that he be named Fernando, after the new president, who was inaugurated today, and the mother thought that was a great idea. How many Fernandos were born today is anyone's guess. Probably some Fernandas were born as well.

3/26/90: We have great news from this end. While we were eating dinner and talking about what Susan's findings in the qualitative survey meant, a light bulb almost literally went off over her head. All of a sudden, the information she had been gathering coalesced into strikingly clear insights. Susan saw the keys to understanding the symbolic universe of the women here,

247

and it is material that she has not seen anywhere in her readings. If someone providing resources for projects relating to women here doesn't take these understandings into account, the projects will likely run counter to the belief structures of the women and fail. It is fascinating material that pulls together everything Susan has been researching. Conclusions are backed by all the quantitative interviews she has done here and in Lower Calos, plus the qualitative ones she is developing now and the ones she did when we first arrived. Suffice it to say that she is very excited, even waking up in the middle of the night thinking about it. She has worked hard to get to this point, and it is rewarding to see all the effort paying off so well. The long time here has been well spent and resulted in a real breakthrough.

72: Friendly Competition Continues, Part Two

2/10/90: Susan is clobbering Fred in national rummy. In the second set of fifty games, she is ahead, 27–18 already. Fred is hoping to win the next five games to beat her in the combined scores with the first fifty, where he won, 28–22.

2/14/90: The second round of fifty games for the championship of national rummy of Brazil ended last night, with Susan winning 29–21. After one hundred games, she has a slight edge, fifty-one games to forty-nine games, but total points of both rounds give the edge to Fred, with a remarkably close thirteen thousand five hundred forty-seven to thirteen thousand five hundred fifty-four (low points wins). The third round will be a real test.

3/09/90: The third round of the national rummy championship has begun, and Fred has roared out to a great start.

4/07/90: We are into the third rubber round of the national rummy tournament. We are tied, 7–7. Susan has come back from 7–2. But it is still a long way to fifty games.

73: It's About Time

2/13/90: The time has switched back to the usual hour now. No more "summer schedule." This has been a fight for the last four months. Since the days here near the equator are fairly constant, a need for daylight savings time is unclear. But they like it in Rio, so every year there is a fight about this issue. There are really two times here – the official hour, and the hour everyone goes by. Whenever you set something up with someone, you have to clarify which hour they are going by. Ceará unilaterally declared that the state was returning to the old hour, but the court ruled that was illegal, so we've changed the official hour four times now. At least that's over.

2/14/90: Happy Valentine's Day! Today we are marking our one-year anniversary of our arrival in Upper Calos, when we walked into a house that had been vacant for more than three years. The house was filthy, damp, leaking, bug-infested and surrounded by weeds. It is hard to take in how much it has changed. Neither Valentine's Day nor our one-year anniversary has drawn much local attention, which is surprising, as every excuse becomes a holiday.

We had another twenty-four-hour power outage, from Monday at five p.m. until yesterday at about five fifteen p.m. Fred had to cook everything that we had, so he was in the kitchen most of the afternoon. Luckily, there wasn't too much, because we've allowed supplies to dwindle, with our trip coming up.

Once the repairmen got to it, it took them only ten minutes to fix the power outage. That was all it took. We can see what is likely to happen during *Carnaval*, when we won't be able to find anyone to fix an outage.

The desire to have the romance of candlelight dinners has greatly diminished. Candlelight dinners will have a completely different connotation from here on.

74: Turn at the Cashew Tree

2/09/90: On February 16 we go to Fortaleza and then plan to take a short excursion to Natal, about six hundred kilometers east. We will visit some old cities and see one of the top beaches of Brazil. Fred will see if we can find a sculptor for making masters for toy soldiers. We will get a new view for a while. We should be back here by February 23. *Carnaval* follows on the 24th, so we want to be home safe and sound before that. Everything closes for at least five days. Some places even close for the week and the weekends. This includes banks. We will be sure to be well stocked with dollars to survive the week.

2/14/90: We leave for Fortaleza tomorrow and then on to Natal, from where bombers flew to North Africa, as part of air-power build-up during World War II. Natal is on the easternmost bulge of Brazil. It was a shorter hop to Europe from Natal than from the U.S. Vaneza and Regina will go with us as far as Fortaleza, where Regina's sister lives in the peri-urban area.

2/24/90: To get to Regina's sister's house, Regina's mother gave us directions that we found astounding. "Locate the Ceará factory, then go down the highway a little more, turn at the cashew tree and then ask for Neto" (the sister's husband). Turn at the cashew tree! For a big city like Fortaleza, we thought these directions were far from compelling. They seemed more suited to locating a house in a rural area, rather than a city of 1.8 million.

Indeed, it took us two hours to find the house, although we did find a cashew tree almost immediately.

First of all, Brazilians don't know each other by name in the city. We asked all around the neighborhood, but no one knew a Neto, which is a fairly common nickname in Brazil. We drove down some alleys – all dirt roads but with some big dirt lumps – and put a hole in the fuel line, which was ingeniously patched at the nearest gas station for less than a dollar. The mechanic had a plastic tube that was too big around to use as a sleeve, so he put it in a fire and melted down the ends until the tube made a tight fit. The tube is still on the fuel line, working fine. In our time in Brazil, we have found auto mechanics to be the most ingenious people. They always find a way to make a car work.

As the car was being fixed, Regina remembered that part of the directions was that the house was within hearing range of music from a "club" in the middle of the neighborhood. We found the club, but that didn't seem to help at all. We had no last name, as we did not know the last name of the son-in-law, since everyone in Brazil goes by first names or nicknames. But we knew the name of the factory where Neto worked. So, we went to the factory and found out that over five thousand people work there, including a couple of hundred men who go by the name Neto. When we could provide no last name, the guards just rolled their eyes. (We found out later that the son-in-law had been laid off anyway.)

Finally, we went to a store where Regina's cousin works; he led us on his bike to his home, where we picked up another cousin, who knew where the house was. It turns out that we had passed the house three or four times and had even made inquiries at a store that was about one hundred feet from the house. It was indeed within hearing distance of the "club." We also found the infamous cashew tree, right where Regina's mother said it would be. For a person with a rural mentality, the directions were perfect. This episode was a genuine contrast between how people from the city (the two of us) and the country perceive reality.

Here is another example of local knowledge: At one point early in Susan's research we sat with one family who, without leaving their chairs, told us about all one hundred forty houses in the entire district, where they were and who lived in them. This saved Susan a long mapping exercise. When she went to the houses to do interviews, the mapping data proved to be accurate. Memories of non-literate people can be impressive.

75: Surrealism

2/24/90: After three nights in Fortaleza, we left for Natal on Monday. We spent a night at a hotel at the halfway point, in the town of Mossoró, now known to us as Moscaró (*mosca* meaning fly) because of all the flies in the hotel. The town had one attraction. Petrobras, the state-run oil company, had been drilling in the area and struck a hot spring at almost one thousand meters. A pump was hooked up to it, and now water gushes to the surface at almost the rate of one hundred forty-four thousand liters per hour and hits the surface at one hundred thirty-four degrees. To take advantage of this, Petrobras has linked up ten pools, running off the water from the first pool, the hottest, in open-air conduits of various lengths to the other pools, so that each pool is a slightly lower temperature, since the water cools as it moves down the conduits. But even the coolest pool was eighty-four degrees, still a bit warm to stay in it for very long. Susan tried each one, the hottest only with her foot.

We had a good dinner at the restaurant, though the flies were fierce. Fred killed a dozen flies and more mosquitoes in our room. Fortunately, we had brought the electric fan with us, so we passed the night well, but we wouldn't go back there.

The "ocean" drive to Natal was as much as sixty kilometers inland. We had to detour to get to the beach road, which was hilly but straight as an arrow, sometimes going from horizon in rear to horizon in front. The next day, we stopped off at two beaches, one of them of worldwide fame, but again we were very disappointed. The famous one was loaded with beachcomber/hippie/foreign types.

We had a surreal experience. We were ready for lunch and walked into a restaurant. One person indicated a table where we could sit. Though it was noon, no one else was in the place. That should have been a hint. We sat. Soon a woman came up and politely asked what she could do for us. We asked what they had to eat, and she replied that there was nothing to eat. We asked for something to drink, and she said that they had nothing to drink, either, but that if we waited, the restaurant next door would open in a little while. In Brazil, "a little while" can have various meanings. She said she highly recommended the other restaurant. We decided to leave.

We walked a little out on the edge of the dune overlooking the sea and saw a beautiful, long "scimitar" beach backed by huge dunes from one point of land to another. You had to walk or ride a beach buggy to get down to the beach, and it was way too hot and a bit too weird to stay.

On the way to the car we talked to an elderly lady who was making lace. She said she had lived there her whole life, then pointed to her mother, who started out as eighty-eight years old but by the end of the conversation was ninety-seven. She had also lived there her whole life.

We decided to move on to the next town, a fishing village, and there at least we could drive down to a beach road, which had restaurants along it on one side and fishing boats on the other. We had a nice conversation with the woman who was the cook and owner. We felt a bit more on earth. A fishing boat came in and unloaded its catch. Everyone was Brazilian. There were no slick types. It was much more the real Brazil we have come to know.

The drive was uneventful except for the wasp that hit the wing window on the right side with a splat, shot behind Fred's back on the ricochet and stung him on the shoulder about ten seconds later. It got Fred good, and he is still swollen. Curiously, on the return trip he flicked another wasp off his neck as he was driving. He had never had that happen before. It is scary, because it distracts you from the driving. We got into Natal and, contrary to Susan's first experience there in 1987, found it to be a fine place, much nicer than hot, dirty Fortaleza. It is smaller than Fortaleza and much better organized. We happened upon a comfortable three-star seaside hotel and settled in after negotiating a thirty percent discount because we were paying in cash.

Fred had seen a sculptor's work in Fortaleza that he thought was exceptional and particularly suited to making masters from which to craft molds for lead figures. We had the address of the sculptor, and since it was close to Natal, we spent the next morning locating him and talking business. He was very friendly and called in his son, who has an interest in doing military figures. For the first time since we have been here, Fred saw someone's eyes light up with ideas. The son was genuinely excited about giving it a try, ready to go to the library to do research, all set to go. Fred had pictures to show him. Fred now has some of the plastic cowboys and Indians and will send them to him as examples. The son said he would have something ready for Fred in two weeks. We will start with some of the historical figures of Brazil first. That will bring newness to the U.S. toy soldier market. It could be the start of a long partnership.

The father was so proud of his work, getting out the scrapbook and showing us his shop. He makes all the figures from scratch out of clay. Fred would have sworn he used a mold! It was a good experience, nice to see someone with such a sense of quality.

2/25/90: We decided to travel all the way back to Fortaleza in one day, about five hundred thirty kilometers. The car did very well, and the roads held out on the different route we tried. Just a bit outside of Fortaleza we hit the first official rains of the rainy season, according to the satellite picture of global weather, with clouds building up over Africa and then rolling this way. It makes the world seem small. We reached Fortaleza in six hours, not driving over ninety kilometers per hour, since the car might fall apart if we go over that.

The next morning, we went to the place where we bought the car, to see if our salesman could give us an idea about the value and way to sell the car. The best news of the whole trip is that he said we could sell it for NCz$180,000 (we paid NCz$4,300 last February). This comes to about only $300 less than we paid for it. With the threatened shortage of alcohol, the state of the car, and our experience with used and old cars in the States, we weren't prepared for the nice surprise. The market apparently is very tight, particularly for used cars, and the value of cars is going up faster than inflation, eighty-two percent versus seventy-three percent last month alone. In addition, Ceará "exports" alcohol to other states, so it should not suffer from shortages, according to the dealer. The governor cut off shipments to other states to make sure that his state has enough alcohol. The money will certainly help offset the cost of a new car when we return to the States.

The trip back to Upper Calos from Fortaleza was uneventful. We picked up Regina and Vaneza at the house by the cashew tree and hit the second day of rains almost all the way. Lower Calos received seventy-two millimeters and made the national news for it. The house was nice and dry when we got home, as Raimundo had done some more roof repair. We think we are snug for the season now.

76: Another Death in the Family

3/06/90: One weekend shock in the community was the sudden death of Raimundo's mother. His father died six months ago after a long illness. His mother died probably instantly, at home, of unknown causes but most likely a heart attack. It's easier to go quickly but harder on the family perhaps. Raimundo came by, very broken up, and asked for money for the coffin. He had already collected some money from the owner of his *sítio* and had received other money as well. We gave him enough to complete the price of the coffin plus a bit extra, in all about U.S. $8.50 equivalent. The coffin seems to run about $20.

We went to the vigil of the body Sunday night, which took place in Raimundo's family home, the same place where we had seen Raimundo's father laid out. The house is quite humble – two rooms with a dirt floor and six hammocks strung up. In the middle of one wall, right over the head of the body, a child had drawn men in blue-and-gray clothes, some on horses and some walking. The drawings were there last time, so they must be part of the permanent wall fixtures. As before, candles were laid out on tables around the body, except the wind kept blowing them out. This was the third wake we have attended. It seems bodies are always laid out with their feet to the door. People approaching the house or standing outside can view the body. The coffin is a wooden framework with a brown plastic sheet spread out over the frame and stapled on.

Rain was threatening, and this area had no electricity, but people were arriving at a steady pace. They entered the small front room, said a prayer over the body and either took a seat in one of the three chairs or on a bench or went back outside to talk. The chairs are too narrow for Fred; he is always getting caught between the arms. The vigil is all night long, with mostly the men of each visiting family staying behind. Dogs and cats wandered in and out, a rooster crowed right outside the door and children ran around. We stayed about fifteen minutes. Others came and went almost right away. Still others had obviously been there a while.

Fred went into Santa Rosa early Monday to have the car fixed before the funeral. He came back with a much quieter and more respectful car. We drove back to the funeral house at about one p.m., just in time for the removal of the coffin from the house. Raimundo was very distraught, airing his grief in a loud voice that could be heard by those outside the house. We think he took it harder than the rest of the family, though all the sons were upset. One son was clearly drunk, as were several other men.

One of the passenger trucks had been arranged to carry the mourners, but in the car we took Raimundo, his wife Teresa, their daughter Julia and two girls we didn't know. We followed the truck, which was loaded over the sides with people, in addition to the coffin. A man to the front of the truck's bed carried a black cross about two and a half feet long. It had the name of the deceased and the date of death painted on it in white letters. People were picked up along the way, the majority being men, as it is customary for the women to watch the body leave the house but not go to the ceremony.

When we got to town, two women were sweeping the church and left a huge pile of dirt right where the coffin was to be set.

Susan asked one of them if she was going to clean it up, and the woman said she would do it afterwards! The other one took the hint, and they picked the pile up. The coffin was reopened and placed on a bench set in the back of the church. Raimundo had to find someone to say the prayers over the body, since the priest wasn't in town. One of the nuns obliged, though she called the deceased by the wrong name the whole time. At the end, she sprinkled holy water over the body and got out of the church rudely fast.

A cart is typically arranged to carry the coffin up the hill to the cemetery, but no cart was there. The men thus took turns carrying the coffin. During the search for the nun, some of the men had taken advantage to drink a bit more, and it showed. One older man we know well, who had just come off a week-long binge the day before, used that chance to start up again.

The walk to the cemetery was quickly accomplished to the accompaniment of the church bell, which served the purpose of calling people to their windows to watch the procession and find out who had passed away. An old woman was obviously glad it wasn't she who had passed away. One of the pall bearers was drunk and provided all the verbal instructions you could possibly need for the job. Fred stayed a little back with Alfredo while everyone entered the cemetery. Fred looked back down the path and saw a group of men passing the bottle. Alfredo commented, "*O negócio da cana!*" (That business with liquor!)

At least the hole in the ground had been prepared. Two men jumped down and, after opening the coffin again for Raimundo to see his mother one last time, they set the coffin on the bottom, again with the help of the unneeded instructions. Everyone then threw a handful of the red dirt on the coffin, and three men started to cover it with dirt. Sadly, one of the shovelfuls uncovered a skull that had evidently come out of the hole with the dirt. The men nonchalantly shoveled the skull back into the hole.

We got back to the car in front of the church and waited for our passengers to return, which took about twenty minutes. Raimundo was still shaken, but the community support plus the liquor seemed to help him somewhat. In all, the ceremony only took a couple of hours.

3/09/90: Anthropologists must be good observers and writers, with an ability to see and describe in simple terms. Fred has been reading some of Susan's anthropology books and has seen a style that he is trying to emulate a bit in these letters, particularly in the descriptions of events. The funeral description is his longest try, and he enjoyed writing it.

77: Powerless

3/09/90: Fred is going to put his film in the refrigerator in the lead pack and also inside a ziplock bag. With the power outages, the fridge often gets wet. Since Saturday, we have had an outage every day, ranging from about twenty to thirty seconds' duration to one of over eight hours. The eight-hour one defrosted the freezer for us.

3/26/90: Raimundo came by on Sunday. The power had been out locally since ten p.m. Saturday. He asked if we wanted to put anything in his freezer, since his refrigerator has finally arrived and is installed at his *bodega*, which is outside our *sítio* and on a different line and so still had power. That's the first time that someone has thought we might have a problem and offered a solution without our asking. It was very nice.

3/29/90: It seems like 1890! We are sitting by candlelight again. The power went to brown light about eight a.m., which isn't sufficient to run the refrigerator or the fan. Then at about four p.m., it all went out when a storm hit. It's now eight p.m., and we are seeing a lot of lightning toward Santa Rosa. Fred has placed some of the falling ice from the freezer back on top of the meat. We hope he won't have to cook all of it.

3/30/90: We stayed in 1890 until eleven thirty a.m. No classes last night, although all the students went, waited about half an hour and then were sent home. Fred didn't go into town, since his class doesn't start until eight thirty. The trucks carrying the students had already passed by our house on the way home by then. Fred had to cook two chickens today, but the other meat seems to have come through fine. You just can't live a twentieth-century life here unless you have a generator, and we don't. The folks without electricity at all probably do better. You can't be frustrated or disappointed if you have no expectations.

4/24/90: We had a power outage Saturday night. It began at eleven thirty and didn't end until ten a.m. Monday. We also had a one thousand percent increase in our electricity bill (from seventy-two to over nine hundred *Cruzeiros*), and the guy wouldn't come out on Sunday to check on the outage unless someone drove him out and back and slipped him something under the table. Fred wasn't in on the discussion. We have decided to let the Brazilians get angry about this stuff – for a while they were counting on us to solve the weekend power-outage problem. Though Fred would have thrown a fit with the power guys, none of our Brazilian friends took this on.

78: International Women's Day

3/11/90: We are all happily ensconced in the main room. Romey is rocking with Susan in the hammock. Fred is at the table. It is dark out, and, as we remember from last rainy season, the mosquitoes (gnats) come out in force from about four p.m. on. True to form, they did today, so we are inside.

It has been a busy day. To commemorate International Women's Day, the women of the community organized a procession from one of the close-by *bodegas* to the local church here in our *sítio*. It was supposed to begin at eight a.m., but they changed the time to nine. Regina asked that we get a message about the time change. We didn't get the news but decided to go at eight thirty anyway, because things here so often start late; it didn't start until nine forty-five.

The procession was nice. Many of the women sang a hymn. They marched behind a street-wide banner. Some women were assigned to carry symbols of their lives as women. One carried beans and a hoe. Another, a pregnant woman, carried a child in her arms. A third was the symbol of a widow. Still another carried a mop and bucket. It was interesting to see what symbols they selected. No one represented a hat maker, which they all do for a great proportion of their time. Part of Susan's research involves the symbolic life of women, and this was right in that area. Susan's early research finds that women see themselves as strong and men as weak; women as blood and men as water – good stuff.

After filming the procession, Fred went to Upper Calos town to film the distribution of hoes to the workers, brand-new blades that the workers were carrying as Fred entered town. A mass was in progress in the volleyball court, and it was HOT. The priest gave a twenty-five-minute sermon. Men held the hoe blades up to give themselves some shade. The priest was under the shade of an umbrella. Fred met the head of SUCAM for the state of Ceará. SUCAM is the government agency in charge of public health measures that involve the environment, principally spraying. It sprays for mosquitoes that carry dengue and other diseases and is generally in charge of disease control. The official was here as a guest of our agronomist friend. Fred invited the official to stop by our house on his way out of town. Fred brought two men from our *sítio* who were at the mass and wanted a ride. They were well into their cups.

The SUCAM man came by soon after. He was here for about an hour. We had a good conversation. He was very interested in Susan's research.

79: Drink Responsibly

3/26/90: One of our neighbors gave himself a real black eye (figuratively) on Sunday afternoon when he got drunk, got into an argument at Alfredo's *bodega*, went home and returned with a sickle (*foice*) and started waving it around and grabbing one guy by the hair. Naisa had made lunch for a good-sized group of customers. They had eaten, but the drunken neighbor scared them all off. Alfredo is furious at the drunk, who doesn't remember a thing, or so he says. This type of incident happens a lot here. We are finding out that many of those crosses along the sides of the road are marking deaths caused by knife fights as well as car accidents. The situation could have been a lot worse, since one of the people the drunken man was calling names and insulting was out of earshot; supposedly this other man carries a revolver. He himself had gotten lit last week and shot at the statues in the town square in Upper Calos. The police did nothing. The local liquor they make from sugarcane here is dangerous. The fermentation period is literally only three or four days.

80: The Third Time is the Charm!

3/30/90: Romey has been fairly sick with a cough, runny nose and an eye infection that looks like pink eye. She also had a high fever. The young women who work with us blamed it on a curse a woman, who people allege has evil-eye power, supposedly put on Romey by saying how cute she was a few too many times. So, Romey received the following treatments: a shot of penicillin, some tea made from flowers that the nurse retrieved from behind the health post, and a set of prayers recited three times over Romey by a woman we were told to ask to see Romey, as she has the power to counter evil-eye curses. For whatever reason, Romey is better today!

81: Feeling at Home

4/04/90: We got a lot done in Fortaleza. We had car trouble, which caused an ugly overcharging incident. We paid out too much money for everything. So much so that Fred found himself on our back steps when we got home, saying – without thinking – "How good is this!" Then he immediately thought about how he had been complaining about aspects of our life in Upper Calos. But compared to Fortaleza, it was a relief to get home! The air is cooler, clouds were pouring over the hilltop behind us and then swirling around the house, we had electricity, and the coolness was keeping the bugs down. Not a bad environment.

4/10/90: It's teatime! Fred went out back and picked a lime off the tree to squeeze into his tea. This is the time of day we love – that stretch from four to six p.m. when things are cooling down, a light breeze is blowing, and the colors have a tinge of "burnt umber" (remember that crayon?). If the bugs are lying low, it is very pleasant.

4/13/90: Today is Good Friday, our second one here. People have been coming up all morning – about fifty kids so far and three adults – to collect *ismola*, a Good Friday offering in the trick-or-treat tradition, though no trick is associated. We have cookies, bananas and some chocolate candies, the latter only for kids we know well. So, we have come full circle, as Judas should go up a tree again tonight if a replacement can be found for the tree that fell last year. Recall that last year Judas got his revenge by taking out a power line. Last year we were suspicious of everything in a "it's all so new to us" sense and "not to be taken advantage of" sense also. This year we understand it and enjoy it. Attitude development is interesting.

4/16/90: Many of the men who had migrated to São Paulo for work are coming home. What this means is that the items they produced in São Paulo to be shipped for sale in the *bodegas* are unlikely to be replaced once sold off the shelves. It's the start of a vicious cycle. It is better for families to be together, but there are no jobs to be had here in Upper Calos, and the migration back home will encourage employers here to keep the wages at an even lower level, since workers are plentiful. The owner of the hotel under construction gave a raise to the neighbor who is a foreman of sorts for the hotel, on the condition that he say nothing about it to anyone else. That is the way things are done here.

Susan recently received a letter from a professor who is a specialist in Brazil. In only a few phrases, he demonstrated his wealth of understanding of Brazil. "Say what you will, there are too many established interests against change." This is something we have seen, but, as optimistic control-your-own-destiny Americans, we have a hard time accepting. But he is right. And, as pessimistic as it sounds, Brazil is not going to change, the new president notwithstanding. This realization, which we are slowly having to accept, is adding a layer of sadness to what has been an amazing experience here.

4/18/90: We will miss several things about this place. The people have been very friendly and open, particularly the women with Susan. She will be leaving several friends behind. Fred has found that he still has an aversion to *machismo*, which seems to be in almost all the men, so he hasn't gotten close to anyone here. The other day, he was returning from buying some bread at

Alfredo's *bodega*, and Susan asked him who was there. He replied, "Nobody – just the guy who beats his wife every weekend when he gets drunk, the guy who pulled a knife on another guy when he was drunk, and the guy who carried a gun and shot up the statues in Upper Calos town the other week when he got drunk." People who don't live here often comment to us about how quiet life here must be. To the contrary, life here is never dull. They have no idea. That is a preconceived notion that some urban and more affluent people have about the rural poor.

4/21/90: We had a good rainy day yesterday. As Fred sat at the table in our main room, the steam was rising from the cobbles of the parking area for about fifteen minutes, the heat of several days getting a release. Today is cloudy and cool. Fred had planned to try to play volleyball, but the court is certainly awash. Susan is in Lower Calos to deliver the prizes from the lottery she held for the interview participants. This is the last time that she has to cart a full load of people around. We hope the car holds up.

82: The Fragility of Tenure

4/07/90: Yesterday, as Fred was standing on the back "porch," thinking to himself how nice everything was, Susan came out and told him about a family she knows well that is getting kicked out of their house by the landowner. The landowner lives in Fortaleza. The daughter of the to-be-evicted family had been working for the landowner there for the last two years. Regina recounted to Susan many ways the landowner has been mean to the daughter, culminating with the threat to evict her family if the young woman ever left their employ. Well, she found a better job in another home in Fortaleza and did leave their employ. The landowner found her, took back the few things he had given her (a bed sheet and a few other things), drove her home here, charging Crz$200 (she was only making Crz$500, less than $10, per month with them) and told the family they had to be out by next Wednesday, in five days. It seems they still have slavery here!

Though plenty of basic houses in Upper Calos town are empty, in town there is rent to pay and no land to work. One pretty much enters the cash society with a move to town, so a job is a necessity. Houses on *sítios* are harder to find and mean moving some distance, often away from friends and family.

Well, we decided to see how we could help out the family about to be evicted. We let them know that we were willing to help them move or help in some other way. The landowner found out that we knew about the eviction and that we were going to help the people any way we could. The landowner returned from Fortaleza and changed his tune a bit. He told the family that they could stay until they found another place to live. The situation is still ugly, but much better for the family, since they will not have to settle for just anything. Now at least the family has some time.

The turn of events demonstrates that the landowner knows that his behavior is wrong and highhanded and that it looks bad to pull these stunts in front of "the Americans." It must be that some of the neighbors of the family used our knowledge of the situation to advantage to help the family out. Everyone says that it was because we knew what was happening that caused the landowner to soften a bit. It also shows that the *moradores* know their landowners well and know what levers to pull. It is further evidence that appearances are important here. If our presence has done no other good, we have at least helped in this case.

83: Raimundinha and Her Sieves

4/13/90: Today is a beautiful, quiet day. It is just the three of us in the house. The bugs are a nuisance, but that can't be helped. Whoops. Fred spoke too soon. Raimundinha just came by. She is a real character, a challenge to describe. She is a dark-skinned older woman, very thin and with a curious voice. She comes around when she needs something – usually money. Susan cleverly put her to work. Raimundinha makes baskets and sieves – those flat ones we have on our wall here in the house. So, Susan ordered some to take home to the U.S. and paid her in advance. The woman is really a piece of work. The first time we saw her, she was poking around our windows. Now we think she is just curious. Susan even likes her. I took some photos of her.

84: A Fifteenth Birthday Party

4/15/90: This evening we went to a fifteenth birthday party, our third such event here. It was in a *sítio* with a small clump of houses down the road we used to run on. The affair was very simple yet very nicely done, with about fifty to sixty guests. The father was serving out of his private stock of *cachaça*. He served it in four choices of drink: *vinho* (wine); *maizena* (a "licor"); *bati-bati* (like a Screwdriver with *maracujá* fruit juice); and *puro* (pure). The whole little cluster of houses in the *sítio* is closely knit, with many of the people related. Fred sat back, out of the way with the men, and just watched. The party was low-key but fun. Now we have seen a rich person's fifteenth birthday, a middle-type (ours for Vaneza) and a very modest one, just on the edge of not being able to support having a party at all.

One of the neighbors had made little pink baskets for the party, bunny faces cut out, colored and pasted on, with paper shreds and three pieces of candy, each individually wrapped. A bamboo frame extended from the front of the house with a canvas roof and about ten balloons. Paper bunting stretched out very low. Fred kept having to duck. All the chairs from the neighborhood were set facing in from the edge. The setting gave an impressive display of faces – from the very old to babies. There was dancing inside the house to *forró* music. At first, just the six- to eight-year-olds danced, and then at about nine thirty, the older kids kicked in. We don't think the older group ever joins in!

4/16/90: Regina stayed at the party until one thirty a.m. It appears there was another party after the birthday party. Regina is young, but she still looks a little worse for wear today. Why do they have these things on a work night?

85: An Affair to Remember

4/24/90: We have scheduled a good-bye party here for May 5. We are making silk-screened invitations with the Brazilian flag and the American flag, their flag poles crossed. The party starts at seven p.m. and, contrary to Brazilian custom, we put an end time on it: eleven p.m. Sometimes, partygoers don't even arrive until eleven, so we specified the end time to protect ourselves. We plan to hand-deliver about one hundred fifty invitations, though probably one half will show up. The cost will be high – U.S. $200 or so – but we think it will be a nice way to say thanks and to depart the community with grace. We know that our friends here can't afford to give us any type of a good-bye party, so to relieve that anxiety, we have told everyone that it is the custom in the U.S. for the people who are leaving to organize and pay for such a party themselves. Our friends will contribute a lot in kind with their help.

5/08/90: The party went great; over two hundred fifty people attended, from the mayor and entire town council to the poorest of the poor. And we thought only about seventy-five or so people would turn up! Though we had been warned by our friends that people who had learned about the party but had not received an invitation were likely to show up, we did not anticipate what occurred.

Early in the event, the local bus pulled up at the bottom of our drive and disgorged dozens of people from town, only to return to town, pick up more people and come back with another load. The Brazilian custom of a hello kiss on each cheek chapped the lips of both of us, as we met and greeted the people who got off the bus and walked up to the house.

We felt like we had spent the whole first half of the evening kissing people hello and the whole second half kissing people good-bye. We didn't even know some of the people who came. But they knew us.

We were very worried that it would rain the night of the party, since it had rained every day and part of every night for about three weeks until last Thursday, when for some nice reason the rains stopped. It turned out that we had a beautiful night for the party. In addition, we had had power outages every Saturday night for the last month. So, Fred very cunningly visited our local power company in Santa Rosa and invited the workers there to our party. They promised not to turn the power off on the night of our party, and – miracle of miracles – there was no problem. Of course, a couple of the power company workers showed up, too.

We had visited the beer distributor in Santa Rosa the week before, someone we had grown to appreciate and enjoy, to order delivery of the beer and soft drinks for the party (we had learned early on that arrangements like this have to be made face to face). He surprised us when he offered twenty metal folding tables and eighty chairs for use at the party – to be delivered to our home for free along with the drinks. The delivery was on time, and we spread the tables out over the parking area. We reserved the veranda for the bar and dancing, and we served food out of the main room of the house.

People were invited to take a seat at a table as they arrived. This caused quite a bit of astonishment among the poor who attended, since they are not accustomed to such hospitality from people who are better off. We soon ran out of seating. What caused even greater astonishment as the night wore on was that we did not ask poor people to vacate their seats for richer people who arrived later. The American principle of "first come, first served" was the order of the evening. If the better-off neighbors minded, they did not show it. They mingled well with the other partygoers.

We went through ten cases of beer in liters, ten cases of soft drinks and a dozen batches of the spiked punch *bati-bati*. Our neighbor women saw that, with such numbers arriving, the food would run out by mid-party, so we abandoned the idea of a serve-yourself buffet (which would have been an American mistake). Friends had warned that people who had very little might heap their plates to the fullest and even take food home in their pockets. The women all pitched in to shred the chickens and even put portions of food on each plate. Nonetheless, despite our best attempts at rationing, early on the food was running out. This is where Third World ingenuity worked a charm. Sônia and Naisa took over and somehow stretched out the remaining food, so that everyone got at least something to eat, even if it was at the end just rice and *farofa*. Susan commented that she could make something out of something, but she couldn't make something out of nothing. Sônia and Naisa managed to do so. All that was left the next day was one bottle of Coca-Cola.

At one point in the party, Fred noticed a familiar face sitting far back in the crowd. Then it dawned on him – it was the *ladrão*, the young man who had tried to break into our car last year and who Fred had knocked down with the twirling softball bat! Fred walked by him, looked him in the eye so that he knew Fred recognized him, and let it all go at that. He was, of course, drinking one of our beers. We think that this encounter attests that everyone was there.

The party was a roaring success, but we needed two days to see straight again. It took all day Sunday to pick up trash and otherwise clean up.

The first comment anyone makes to us about the party is how well it was organized. Second, they say it was an event that they will never forget. Neither will we, but probably for different reasons. People particularly note how we treated all guests as equals. If nothing else, we showed U.S. values in action, and we are proud of that.

In preparation for the party, we rented a jeep for five days – our car could not transport the coolers and other paraphernalia we needed. Fred turned the jeep in yesterday... and that is a relief.

86: The Ups and Downs of Rural Life

5/11/90: This is in the "last straw" category: Susan had agreed to present her preliminary statistical findings to the organization in charge of family planning for Ceará. The time was set for yesterday at two p.m., in Fortaleza. Because of car trouble, Susan had to get to Santa Rosa by truck. She waited at the bottom of our hill for the five fifteen a.m. truck for Santa Rosa, so she could get the seven a.m. bus. The road from Santa Rosa to Fortaleza has deteriorated again, and the trip can take five hours, in what should be a three-hour trip.

The truck didn't come. One came by at six a.m., which was cutting it close, but the seven a.m. bus to Fortaleza was still makeable. Then the truck ran out of gas about five kilometers outside Santa Rosa. Susan was furious. She walked in her dress clothes about three kilometers to the bus station and has the blisters to show for it. She didn't pay the truck driver a thing, missed the bus to Fortaleza, ended up on a local bus that took even longer than five hours, and got to the meeting room just in time. But she had to forgo other things that she had planned to do in Fortaleza. The meeting went well at least, and Susan was able to present some new findings to the group.

Susan caught a bus home that should have put her in Santa Rosa at nine thirty p.m. It arrived at eleven p.m. Transportation had been pre-arranged on a late-night bus that ferries kids to school in Santa Rosa, but it was out of there by ten fifteen, so Susan took a taxi to Dra. Enízia's house in Santa Rosa and slept there. We had agreed that Fred wasn't to get worried until noon today, but even so, it was a relief when Susan pulled up at about ten a.m. in her friend's car. We have it on loan until Monday.

But, in contrast: The other Sunday, Fred was in Upper Calos town and greeted the postman as he passed by. Despite this being his day off, the postman asked Fred if he wanted our mail. So, Fred drove him down to the post office, and he opened up and gave us our mail. This is the type of gesture that can happen in a Third-World setting, where regulations are not so rigid. It is perhaps the counterpoint to the frustrations we have felt sometimes when regulations are not adhered to and that has worked to our disadvantage.

87: Not Well Worth the Trip

5/14/1990: With the trip to Salvador da Bahia an impossibility, we decided to visit Recife, 638 miles away. The trip turned out to be a disaster in every way. We had planned to go by bus, but it was full, so we took our car, with our fingers crossed. We made it to a hotel about two hundred fifty kilometers away, started out the next day, and the car died. Thanks to a fortunate encounter with the people who were staying in the room next to us in the hotel, who just happened to pass us only thirty seconds after the car died, we got transportation to the next town, and they helped to arrange, after a lot of negotiation, a tow to Natal, one hundred twenty kilometers away. From there we could take a bus to Recife. The man with the tow truck wanted to wait a day to tow us, but for an extra $20 he agreed to do it then and there. That was probably a ploy to get more money from us, since most people are eager to take on unexpected paid work. While Susan was in the saviors' car, Fred had to sit in our car to steer and brake, since the "tow bar" attached to our car was only a long rope. Unfortunately, the truck spewed raw hot sticky oil out of its exhaust for the entire trip, splattering the front of the window and the car and adding costs of a thorough cleaning to our repair costs.

5/19/1990: The car is still in Natal, eight hundred kilometers from here. It will cost about $50,000 *Cruzeiros* ($700) to fix. The people who stopped to help are, even as we speak, continuing to assist by keeping on top of a mechanic that they recommended. It is so very comforting when you find you can "rely on the kindness of strangers."

We enjoyed our break in Recife and went back home by bus, including one overnight bus, which was a killer. Fred goes back to Natal by bus on Monday to retrieve the car and try to sell it there. We don't want to subject the car to more travel than minimally necessary. The bus trip to Natal will be about fifteen hours. The people who helped us have done more – much more – than anyone could expect. They live in Natal and have been shepherding the car since its demise.

The revised plans for our final days in Brazil are to stay in Upper Calos until about May 20-22. The "affair to remember" cost about $500, the trip to Recife was and continues to be dear, and we don't feel like experiencing any more travel in Brazil right now. We are exhausted.

5/23/1990: Fred made that last bus trip to Natal and was actually able to sell the car. Our friends there handled the money transaction, and Fred returned with U.S. $500, which we will use as the down payment on a new car when we get back to the States. The legacy of that car will long be remembered. It gave us thirty-two flat tires, four broken motor mounts that required welding, two gas line punctures, several exhaust repairs and replacements, and uncounted hours of unexpected walking due to the car's failure. Fred was not sad to see that car leave our lives. We will not be spending four final days in Fortaleza because of the car fiasco, so this is our last letter home, since any letter sent later will arrive after we do. It is bittersweet to think about leaving after seventeen months in Brazil and sixteen months in Upper Calos. We have had enough struggles and frustrations to risk overshadowing the more pleasant aspects. But if we hadn't been trying to accomplish something, it really wouldn't be so bad here.

88: A Poignant Farewell

5/23/90: We are leaving behind all our possessions, only taking with us our basic clothing. To avoid creating any envy, we have delegated Vaneza to distribute our items after our departure. We have made a detailed list of each item and its intended recipient. Vaneza will show the list to each recipient, so they know she is not depriving them of anything.

Sometimes life here can be very good. The late afternoon can be refreshingly soothing, with the golden light like an early October afternoon in the U.S., the air with a little bit of the heat of the day left over, but not too much, the breeze blowing the branches just enough to provide a general hush for a background and keeping the bugs away at the same time, and the evening birds calling and starting to catch the upward drafts as the land gives off its accumulated heat. Other afternoons provide rain showers, often real downpours. If we have electricity, the downpours can make it downright cozy and sleepy inside the house. We lack only a warm, low fire in a fireplace. Even when the electricity fails, the candles provide their own atmosphere, except that we have had so many candlelit dinners that the romance of that is probably gone forever.

Yesterday afternoon offered a different though equally beautiful vista completely, with clouds rolling in over the hills around us, surrounding us with only one hundred yards of clear vision before they swallowed up everything. We could have been on top of a mountain or on an island two hundred yards in diameter. One time, we saw the clouds flying right at the house, wisps breaking off at the nearby trees and rolling down the hill that is our front yard. If we didn't have a screen on the window, the clouds would have rolled right into the house. It's good to write this down to help us remember the many nice parts of our stay here.

We have learned that it is customary for rural people to say good-bye personally, by walking to a person's house and extending their good wishes face to face. In the days since the party, we have had a steady stream of people coming to our door. Many are people we have not had a direct relationship with. They ask for nothing. They say they have heard of us, know we are leaving and wish to thank us for our contributions to their community. It is very touching because their gift appears to be in the walk the person has made, a type of personal pilgrimage to show respect for the departing person. The exchange with one elderly man was particularly poignant as, hat in hand, he made his way slowly up the cobblestones to our door, having walked quite a distance to say good-bye, even though he had never met us. We greeted him outside our door. He said we had earned his respect and that of other members of the community, and he thanked us. His message delivered, he turned and started his long way back home.

Portuguese–English Glossary for Calos

aguardente   an alcoholic beverage made from sugarcane;
similar to *cachaça*

americanos   Americans

aula de
saudade   a session of school at graduation time that
celebrates the times spent together

bodega   small stores that sell local rum, as well as some
grocery items and household products

cachaça   sugarcane rum, produced locally and sold very
cheap; similar to *aguardente*

cafezinho   a tiny cup of coffee, characteristic of how coffee
is served in Brazil

Carnaval   Carnival or Mardi Gras; celebrated from the
Friday preceding Ash Wednesday until the
following Thursday

casa grande   manor house

centavo   cent, or 1/100 of the prevailing Brazilian currency

287

Cruzado	Brazilian currency unit until January 15, 1989
Cruzado Novo	Brazilian currency unit from January 15, 1989 until March 16, 1990; abbreviated NCz
Cruzeiro	Brazilian currency unit as of March 16, 1990; abbreviated Crz
cururu	giant toad
farofa	manioc (cassava) flour
favela	shantytown
fazenda	ranches, usually specializing in cattle-raising, that are the principal use of land in the *sertão*
fazendeiros	ranchers
feijão	beans, the staple of Northeast Brazil
fim de linha	the place at which the government-supported road ends
foice	hand-held sickle
forró	Brazilian country music originating in the Northeast
fulbito	salon soccer, played with a small soccer ball

-inho, -a	the diminutive suffix, which can connote endearment, cuteness, smallness or youth
ismola	charitable offering; handout
ladrão	thief
loteado	subdivided, as in a subdivision of land
lourinha	blondie; a person with blond hair
mama	the popular term for breastfeeding (noun)
mandioca	cassava, or manioc
mata	woods; bush
mofo	mildew
morador	caretaker or sharecropper who lives on land that is not theirs; often the house they live in also belongs to the landowner
mosca	fly
município	political unit that subdivides states, translated here as municipality or county
Não deu jeito	"It didn't work out"; generic way to say that something did not or could not get done

patrão, -oa	patron, typically a rich person who is a landowner, politician, physician or other professional
perna cabeluda	hairy leg
pescando	literally "fishing," but in school "cheating"
pinga	a synonym for *cachaça*
professor	teacher
quadrilha	harvest dance
Quem não chora não mama	literally, "If you don't cry, you won't get to suckle" – roughly equivalent to "The squeaky wheel gets the grease"
rede	hammock
Região Nordeste	Northeast Region
Se Deus quiser	"If it is God's will"; "God willing"
Semana Santa	Holy Week

sereno   light rain; drizzle

serra   the hills that break up the *sertão*; used here as a
                synonym for Upper Calos

sertão   the hot, dry plain that occupies most of the
                interior of Northeast Brazil; used here as a
                synonym for Lower Calos

sítio   small ranches or farms in the *serra*, known for
                fruit and cashew nuts

tempestad   storm

tranquilo   tranquil; expressed to counsel someone to stay
                calm or have patience

trio eléctrico a musical trio for hire with electronic instruments

vela   spark plug (literally, candle)

velhos   old folks

vereador   town councilman

Printed in the USA
CPSIA information can be obtained
at www.ICGtesting.com
CBHW021113290224
4801CB00008B/112

9 781804 392766